SeaClear Unleashed

ISBN 978-1-4457-2211-5

Typeset in Garamond 12pt

Table of Contents

1. Introduction

What Is SeaClear?

SeaClear is a PC based chart plotter for a PC running Windows up to and including Windows 7. With a GPS correctly connected, SeaClear displays your vessel's current position, speed, heading and other data on the screen. The current chart is automatically repositioned, and new charts loaded. Tracks can be saved to file for later review. Activated routes can be used for navigation or output to an auto pilot and automatically followed.

Included with the SeaClear software package is MapCal, a program which is used to load BSB charts or calibrate scanned image files if needed. This publication, SeaClear Unleashed, includes information on how to use MapCal as it is used to load the charts needed for display and navigation.

 MapCal is the sole method of installing charts for SeaClear. It is included as part of the SeaClear installation. It can be found in the same directory as SeaClear.exe. We recommend that you create a shortcut and move the shortcut to your desktop..

Why SeaClear Unleashed?

SeaClear is a feature rich software package for nautical navigation. The software package includes a SeaClear manual that covers most of the features but is not easy to use. *This* publication, SeaClear Unleashed, has been written by a yachtsman, for yachtsmen and the information contained herein is based on using SeaClear in real life practical situations. It is intended to extend and enhance the original SeaClear manual and realise the software's full potential. It is not the intention of the author to repeat what is already in the original SeaClear manual.

Warning

 This SeaClear Unleashed publication is provided 'as-is', without any warranty, expressed or implied. In no event will the author be held liable for any damages arising from the use of this publication.

How to use SeaClear Unleashed

It is unlikely that any yachtsman will read this manual in its entirety at one sitting. A good start is to read, as a bare minimum, the Quick Start section which get you up and running with SeaClear and your chosen GPS. This publication can then be used as a reference, as and when required.

Each section contains one or more step by step tutorials to simplify the use of SeaClear

We recommend that the hardcopy version of this publication is used, as it can prove difficult to switch to and from SeaClear to view online versions of this publication.

To help you navigate this publication, important information is flagged by margin icons.

The icons used are:

Need to Know

This icon indicates important need to know information that may be safety related or related to the correct use of SeaClear.

Tutorial

This icon indicates a step by step tutorial on the operation of SeaClear. It is possible to get familiar with SeaClear just by closely following all the tutorials in this publication.

2. Quick Start

This chapter is for those of you who do not read manuals. As a bare minimum follow each step by step tutorial to setup SeaClear with a basic configuration to plot you position on a chart and follow a route you create. Once you have done this the rest is up to you to fine tune the display and characteristics of SeaClear by looking at other sections of SeaClear Unleashed.

Quick Install

Tutorial: Install SeaClear to your computer.

In this tutorial you will install SeaClear to your PC will very little difficulty and in a very short time. The installation creates a default installation of SeaClear on your PC.

1. Download the latest version of SeaClear from the www Sping.com . At the **Open File Security Warning** window click **Run** to continue

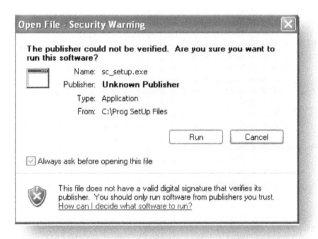

2. At the **Setup** window click **Yes**.

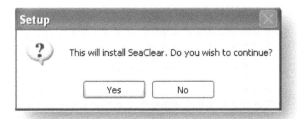

3. At the **Setup SeaClear** window click **Next**.

4. At the **Select Destination Directory** window enter the path to the folder where you would like to install SeaClear or use the down arrow to browse and select an installation folder. Then click **Next**.

5. At the **Select Components** window click **Next**.

6. At the **Select Start Menu Folder** click **Next**.

7. At the **Select Additional Tasks** window click **Next**.

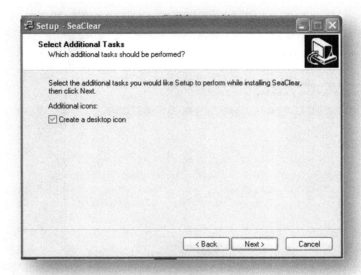

8. At the **Ready to Install** window click **Next** and the installation starts.

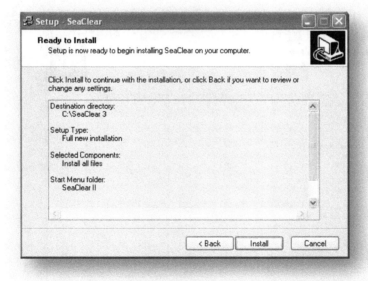

9. At the final **Setup SeaClear** window uncheck the **Open English PDF Manual** checkbox and click **Finish**.

10. This completes a default installation of SeaClear (and MapCal) to your chosen folder. Next you are going to create a shortcut to MapCal on your desktop. Navigate to your SeaClear program folder and locate MapCal

11. Right click on the **MapCal_2** icon and select **Create Shortcut**.

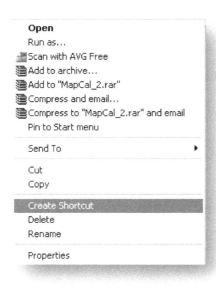

12. A **Shortcut to MapCal_2** is created in the same folder. Right click on the icon and select **Cut**.

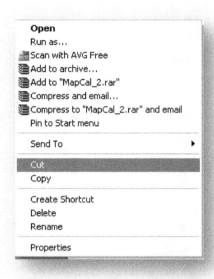

13. Navigate to your desktop and right click and select **Paste**.

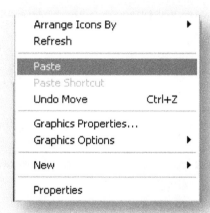

14. A **Shortcut to MapCal_2** is created on your desktop.

Quick Load Charts

Tutorial: Load charts with MapCal

In this tutorial you will load charts to use with SeaClear using the program MapCal. If you have no existing charts you have to download RNC charts from NOAA, purchase BSB charts from a chart vendor or calibrate your own charts using MapCal.

1. Copy any chart **.KAP** files you may have (either downloaded from NOAA, purchased or self calibrated image charts to the **SeaClear/Charts** folder. The folder already contains four SeaClear WCI sample charts.

2. Open MapCal. Select **Tools Set Directories**.

3. Click **Browse** and select the **SeaClear/Charts** folder

4. Click **OK** and the selected folder displays at the **Chart Directories** window.

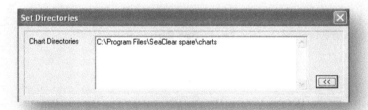

5. Click **OK** and then select **Tools / Autoload List /.Scan for New Charts**.

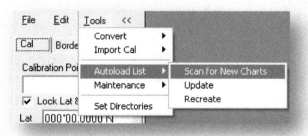

6. MapCal then scans the **Charts** folder and loads any new charts. The number of new charts found displays in the **SeaClear Calibration Utility** window.

7. Click **OK** and then **Exit** MapCal.

Quick GPS Connect

Tutorial: Easily connect your GPS receiver.

In this tutorial you will set up SeaClear with GPS to accurately plot your position, speed and course.

1. Open SeaClear and from the **Tools** menu select **Properties** to open the **SeaClear Setup** window.

2. Select the **Comm.** tab.

3. As communication with a GPS receiver is mainly *input* only, select either **RX2** or **RX3** in the **NMEA Connection** area of the window.

4. Set the **PC Port Com** to match the COM port your GPS unit is using to communicate with your computer. This could be a physical serial port or a virtual serial port.

5. Set the **BPS** (Bits per second) to 4800 (the default speed for GPS)

6. In the **GPS Datum Setting** area, set the datum to match the datum your GPS is using. (Refer to the manufacturers documentation) It is important that the datum set in SeaClear matches the GPS datum, otherwise your plotted position will not be accurate.

7. Click **Save** to save your settings and return to the main **SeaClear** window.

8. Check the setup is ok by selecting **Tools, System, NMEA Input Monitor**, The **NMEA Input Monitor** window the NMEA sentences displayed should include sentences starting with: **$G**   .

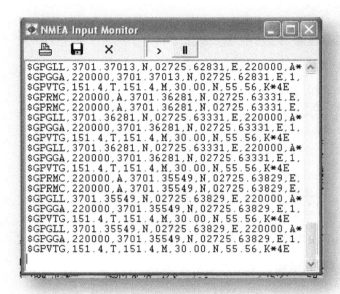

Quick Plot Your Position

Tutorial: Plot your vessel's position.

In this tutorial you will plot your vessels position as reported by your GPS.

1. If the COM ports settings are correct and your GPS is connected and working correctly your vessels position is displayed at the top of the dashboard. Lat and Long displays as well as True COG (**C**ourse **O**ver **G**round) SOG (**S**peed **O**ver **G**round). and Magnetic variation for your position and UTC (**U**niversal **T**ime **C**oordinate) reported by the GPS also display

2. Your vessel's position displays on the chart with a vector for the COG . The vector's length is in proportion to your vessel's SOG. Two distance rings display around the vessel whose radii adapt to fit the screen.

Note: if you have not yet loaded a chart for your vessels position a world chart displays

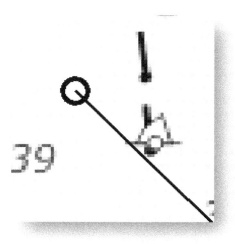

3. Click **Automatic On** and SeaClear automatically follows your vessel's position on the chart.

4. Click **Track On** and your vessel's track plots on the chart.

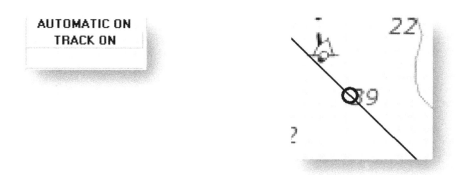

5. As you move the mouse cursor, SeaClear displays the cursor position in Lat and Long and the bearing and distance from your vessel.

```
36°58.879'N
027°26.083'E
201° 1.50nm
```

Note: In this tutorial, SeaClear's default settings have been used which load on installation. Many settings can be user defined such as boat, shape, colour, range rings etc.

Quick Create Route

Tutorial: The easy way to create a route.

In this tutorial you will create a simple route that can be saved followed and modified.

1. With **Automatic Off** select **Tools / Route Editor**.

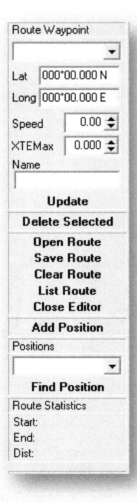

2. In Route Editor mode the cursor displays as below.

3. Double click on the chart to place a way point.

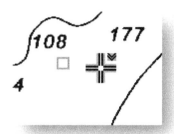

4. The new way point's default name displays in the Route Editor panel.

5. Place two more way points on the chart by double clicking their positions. SeaClear automatically creates route legs between the way points.

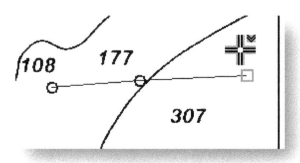

6. Single click on the first way point to select it.. Then enter a name for the way point at the **Name** input box. Click **Update** to apply the new name to the way point.

7. The new name is confirmed at the **Route Waypoint** panel.

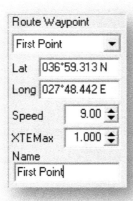

8. Save the route by clicking **Save Route.** At the **Available Routes** window assign the route a name and click **Save**.

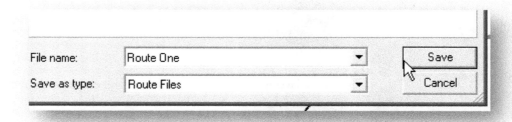

Quick Follow Route
Tutorial: Activate and follow a route
In this tutorial you will activate the route you created

Note: Ensure your vessel is positioned near the first route way point *before* you activate the route. When a route is activated SeaClear sets a course to reduce and eliminate Cross Track Error. If you are too far from the first way point. SeaClear may, under some circumstances, compute a sharp turn to port or starboard. If an autopilot is connected this sharp turn could be hazardous

1. Click **Close Editor** and then click **Activate Route**. When a route is activated SeaClear selects the first leg, which is from way point 1 to 2 and the second way point is highlighted in red. The dashboard displays information to aid navigation. The direction to steer is indicated by the chevrons at the bottom of the route panel.

```
WP-2
BWR      53.0°
XTE      0.17 NM
BOD      85.5°
WCV      25.8kt
RNG      0.3NM
TTG      00:00:39
TRNG     0.9 NM
TTTG     0:04
NEXT     87.3°
TIME     00:00:30

<<<<<<<<<<
```

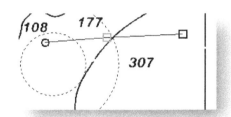

Note: The information displayed:

BWR: Bearing to waypoint, Rumb Line

XTE: Crosstrack error,

BOD: Bearing from Origin to Destinaiton,

WCV: Waypoint Closure Velocity

RNG: Range to waypoint,

TTG: Time to go to waypoint,

TRNG: Range to go end of route,

TTTG: Time to go from current position using waypoint speed data.

NEXT: Next bearing is shown.

TIME: Time since route was activated.

___ | | ___ : Steering indicator, showing how to follow the route.

2. When you vessel arrives at the active way point, the next way point is automatically activated and SeaClear computes the course to this way point.

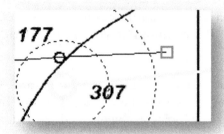
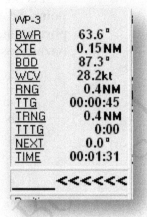

3. De-activate the route by right clicking on the route panel and selecting **Deactivate Route**.

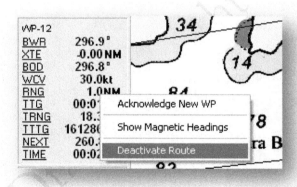

Quick Modify Route

Tutorial: Modify a route

In this tutorial you will extend, and insert new way points in your existing route..In this way new routes can be created from existing routes.

1. Ensure your route is de-activated. Select **Tools, Route Editor** to open the route editor.

2. The cursor displays as shown.

3. Double click near the leg between the first and second way point a new way point is inserted and is automatically named **Way 2** by SeaClear.

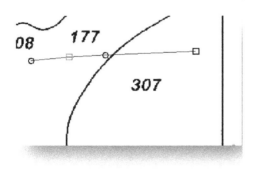

4. Right click on the chart and select **Extend**.

5. Double click some distance from the first way point and a new first way point is created with a leg to the old first way point. If a leg is created to the *last* way point simply right click on the way point your created and select **Delete Waypoint**. Try creating a new way point again, this time further from the old first way point.

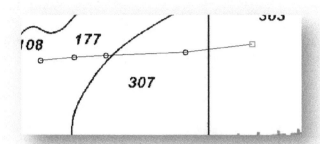

6. Click **List** to display your route in the tabular form. In this form you can rename any, or all of, the way points. Click **Update** and your changes are saved to SeaClear but not yet saved to disk.

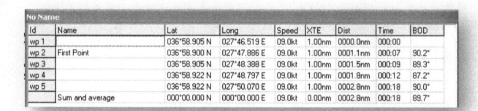

Id	Name	Lat	Long	Speed	XTE	Dist	Time	BOD
wp 1		036°58.905 N	027°46.519 E	09.0kt	1.00nm	0000.0nm	000:00	
wp 2	First Point	036°58.900 N	027°47.886 E	09.0kt	1.00nm	0001.1nm	000:07	90.2°
wp 3		036°58.905 N	027°48.388 E	09.0kt	1.00nm	0001.5nm	000:09	89.3°
wp 4		036°58.922 N	027°48.797 E	09.0kt	1.00nm	0001.8nm	000:12	87.2°
wp 5		036°58.922 N	027°50.070 E	09.0kt	1.00nm	0002.8nm	000:18	90.0°
	Sum and average	000°00.000 N	000°00.000 E	09.0kt	0.00nm	0002.8nm	000:18	89.7°

7. Click **Save** to save the modified route.

3. Using SeaClear

Working with Charts

MapCal is the sole method of installing charts for SeaClear. It is included as part of the SeaClear installation. It can be found in same directory as SeaClear.exe. We recommend that you create a shortcut for MapCal and drop the shortcut on your desktop.

The chart options compatible with SeaClear are;

- Purchase BSB charts from an authorised Maptech reseller.

- Scan an existing paper chart and calibrate with MapCal.

- Download free RNC from NOAA.

- Create your own BSB charts from a scanned image file.

- Download free charts from the internet.

- Download low cost SeaClear compatible charts from a digitising service.

We do not condone the use of charts with SeaClear that infringe copyright or patent laws. Any reference to charts' available on the internet is for information only. We cannot vouch for the legality and or accuracy of charts on the internet. You use such charts at your own legal, and physical, risk.

Downloading charts from NOAA

The NOAA Office of Coast Survey produces nautical charts and related publications for navigation in the coastal areas of the United States and the Great Lakes. NOAA produces two main types of charts:

- RNC (Raster Nautical Charts) These charts are in the raster format BSB which is compatible with SeaClear.

- ENC (Electronic Nautical Charts) These charts are in the vector format and are not compatible with SeaClear.

Tutorial: Downloading RNC charts from NOAA in Eight Steps

In this tutorial you will download from the NOAA web site all the charts for your Coast Guard District for use with SeaClear. The download time may be longer than downloading individual charts, but saves you having to return to NOAA to repeat the individual download process.

1. Use your browser such as Firefox or Explorer to open the page at
    http://www.charts.noaa.gov/RNCs/RNCs.shtml

2. Click on chart name you need. If in doubt click **map** to display a map of Coast Guard Districts.

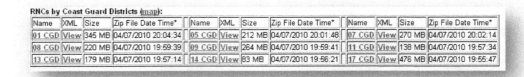

RNCs by Coast Guard Districts (map):

Name	XML	Size	Zip File Date Time*	Name	XML	Size	Zip File Date Time*	Name	XML	Size	Zip File Date Time*
01 CGD	View	345 MB	04/07/2010 20:04:34	05 CGD	View	212 MB	04/07/2010 20:01:48	07 CGD	View	270 MB	04/07/2010 20:02:14
08 CGD	View	220 MB	04/07/2010 19:59:39	09 CGD	View	264 MB	04/07/2010 19:59:41	11 CGD	View	138 MB	04/07/2010 19:57:34
13 CGD	View	179 MB	04/07/2010 19:57:14	14 CGD	View	83 MB	04/07/2010 19:56:21	17 CGD	View	476 MB	04/07/2010 19:55:47

3. Agree to NOAA's Terms & Conditions by clicking **OK**.

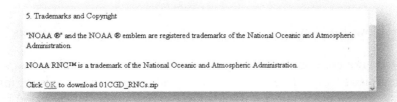

5. Trademarks and Copyright

"NOAA ®" and the NOAA ® emblem are registered trademarks of the National Oceanic and Atmospheric Administration.

NOAA RNC™ is a trademark of the National Oceanic and Atmospheric Administration.

Click OK to download 01CGD_RNCs.zip

4. When prompted by the **Opening ..._RNCs.zip** window select **Save File** and click **OK.**

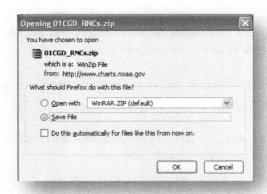

5. Open the saved .zip file with Winzip or Winrar.

6. Click the Extract button and set the folder to match your Charts folder at the Advanced tab set **Paths Off** to prevent the extracted file being grouped in their original folders.

7. Click OK to extract the files to the chosen directory without the directory structure of the zip file.

8. Open your Charts folder to check BSB and Kap files for your Coast Guard District are there.

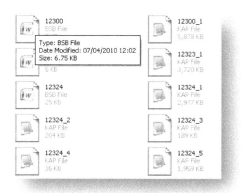

Loading Charts

MapCal is a utility program installed as part of the SeaClear installation process. Charts are only available for SeaClear once they have been loaded via MapCal.

Tutorial: Load Charts for SeaClear Using MapCal in Nine Easy Steps.

In this tutorial you will load charts using MapCal. Once loaded they are available for use by SeaClear. The charts must first of all have been saved, or unzipped, to a known folder

1. Open MapCal.

2. Select **Tools / Set Directories**.

3. At the **Set Directories** window click the browse button <u><<</u> to open the **Browse for Folder** window and select the folder where you have stored, or extracted to, your charts Then click **OK**.

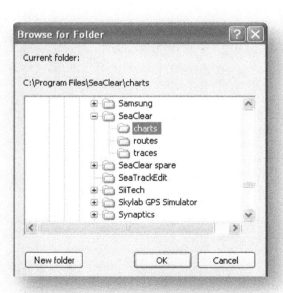

4. At the **Set Directories** window click **OK**.

5. Select **Tools /Scan for New Charts**.

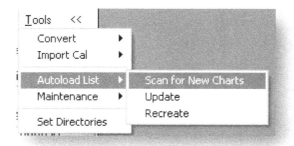

6. Charts found are confirmed by the **SeaClear Calibration Utility** window.

7. Close MapCal and open SeaClear.

8. Select **File**/ **Chart** /**List All**.

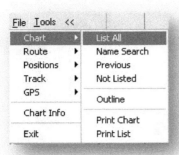

9. All available charts are listed by name, and scale, in the **Available Charts** window.

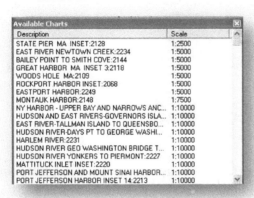

Scanning and Stitching Charts
Tutorial: Scanning and Stitching Charts

In this tutorial you will use a program called Scan n Stitch (http://www.arcsoft.com/estore/software_title.asp?ProductCode=SNSD) to scan a poster sized chart and stitch together the resulting images to form one image file for later calibrating with MapCal.

Note: An alternative to using Scan n Stich is to manually stitch images using a package such as Corel Photo Paint or Adobe Photoshop..

Poster Size Page (Poster/Artwork/Newspaper) Up to 10 scans (2 rows of 5)

1. Align the top left edge of the page on the scanner and click Scan.

2. Scan the entire top edge of the page in overlapping sections. Be sure to use at least 20% overlap.

3. Turn the page around and scan the same way along the bottom side.

Note: For 2-row scanning, top and bottom rows must also have 20% minimum overlap (orange area).

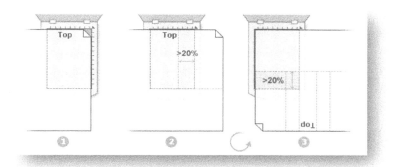

4. Click **Load Files**

5. Use **Ctrl + Click** to select the scanned images.

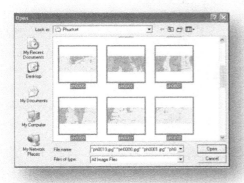

6. The selected images display.

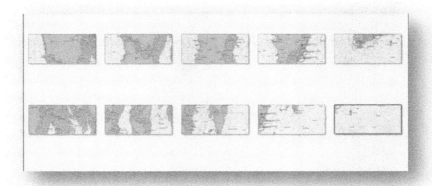

7. Hover over the **Stitch** button and select **Double Row** .

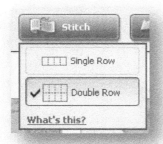

8. The stitching process starts, and progress is reported by the **ArcSoft Scan n Stitch window**

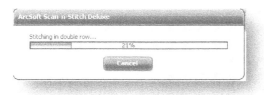

9. The stitched image displays

10. Click **Save Page**.

11. At the **Save As** window browse to the location you wish to use and enter a
    File Name. Select **Save as Type** as **BMP** (The format file format used by
    MapCal) and click **Save**.

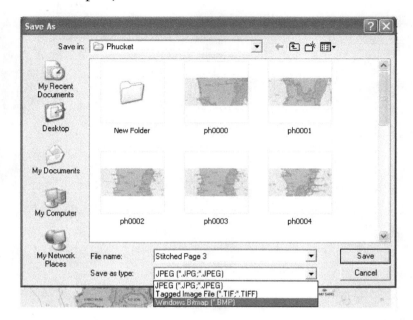

12. Your image has been saved and is ready to be calibrated by MapCal. Go to
    page 37and use MapCal to calibrate your image.

Calibrating Charts

The program MapCal supplied with SeaClear is a utility to convert image files to calibrated charts and convert to the WCI format. To accurately calibrate an image you have to enter the following information:

- The projection of the chart

- The datum of the chart

- The scale of the chart

- A minimum of four calibration points for known positions on the chart

- The border of the chart

Note: If you have scanned a paper chart the projection, scale and datum is printed on the chart. Known positions are normally printed at the corners of the chart.

Tutorial: Calibrating Charts

In this tutorial you will calibrate an image file that you may have downloaded or created by scanning a paper chart. Two versions of the chart are created both of which can be loaded to, and used by SeaClear.

- A calibrated image with is associated calibration file

- A WCI format file that has internal calibration.

1. Open MapCal

2. Select **File / Open Image**

3. At the **Chart Information** window enter

- A **Chart Name** for the chart. This name is used in lists etc.

- The **Scale** of the chart.

- The **Projection** and **Datum** of the chart. Normally Mercator and WGS 84.

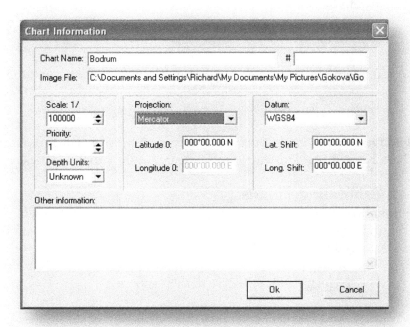

4. Right click on a known **Lat** and **Long** on the chart. For a scanned paper chart this is normally at one of the corners or an intersection point of the printed grid.

5. A calibration point displays on the chart.

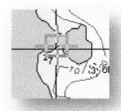

6. At the calibration panel enter the **Lat** and **Long** for this **Point 1**.

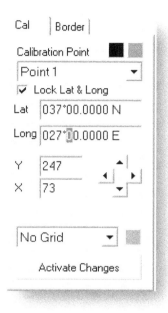

7. Click **Activate Changes** to save this calibration point.

8. Repeat this procedure at least three more times. You will then have created four calibration points at known Lat and Long points of your image.

9. Check the calibration by selecting **Normal Grid** from the grid dropdown box.

10. A grid displays on the charts. The grid should be regular and line up with the chart edges or any existing Lat Long grids.

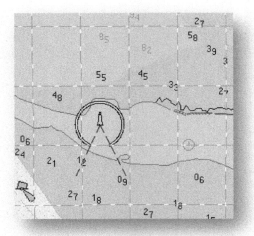

11. Select the **Border** tab and click **Set Border to Image**.

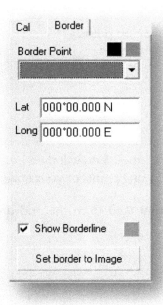

12. Your image is now calibrated. Select **File / Save Calibration**.

13. The calibration for your image is saved as the **CHARTCAL.DIR** file in the same folder as your original image file. The image file itself is unchanged.

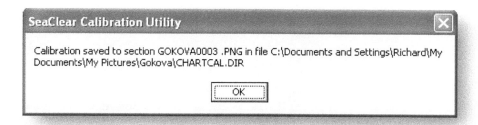

14. Select **Convert** / **Current to WCI**.

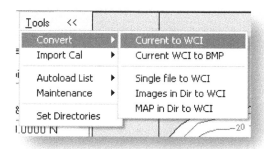

15. Your image file is converted to the SeaClear WCI format. There is no separate calibration file as the WCI file stores the calibration internally. At the **WCI File name** window you are prompted as to where to store your converted file. Browse to your charts folder and click **OK**.

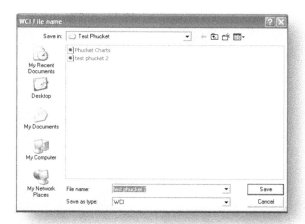

16. The conversion is confirmed at the **SeaClear Calibration Utility** window. Click **OK** to finish the process.

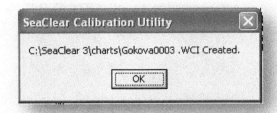

17. The last process is to use MapCal to load this new calibrated chart to SeaClear

18. Go to page 30 and proceed from step 2.

Amending Charts

SeaClear WCI, calibrated image and BSB charts can be amended or updated to reflect changes in local conditions. You may have noted changes to a shallow area or just want to place a favourite watering hole on your chart. Amendments can only be made to an image of your chart. With calibrated image charts you already have the image. With WCI charts, they have to be converted to a bmp image. With BSB charts you can use a utility such as bsb2tif to convert the .kap file of a BSB chart to a .tif image.

Tutorial: Amending a Chart.

In this tutorial you will amend a SeaClear WCI calibrated image or BSB chart.

1. If you want to amend a SeaClear WCI chart, start at step 6 below

2. If you want to amend a calibrated image chart, start at step 8 below.

3. If you want to amend a BSB chart use the utility **bsb2tif**. The utility can be downloaded at: http://libbsb.sourceforge.net/

4. Copy and paste **bsb2tif** to your chart directory.

5. Click the Windows **Start** button and select **Run**. Enter:

```
C:\ProgramFiles\SeaClear\charts\bsb2tif.exe"
xxxx_1.kap  yyy.tif
```

Where xxx.Kap is the name if the BSB charts Kap file to convert, and yyy.tif is the name of the tif image file you want to create. When you have created the tif file proceed from step 8

6. Open MapCal and select **File /Open** image to open the WCI chart you wish to amend.

7. Select **Tool / Convert / Current WCI to BMP** to convert the chart to a BMP image

8. Use any photo editing software to amend either the BMP file, calibrated image file or .tif file.

9. Once you have finished **Save As** a BMP file.

10. The images you have amended may have to be recalibrated. If so recalibrate as shown on page 37

11. Once you have finished calibrating, select **Tools Convert Current to WCI**.

12. Select **Tools / Autoload List / Scan for New Charts**.

13. Your amended chart is now ready for use in SeaClear.

Planning

You may wonder why this section of the publication is longer than the Navigation section on page 57. The secret to successful, and safe, navigation is preparation. There is an old saying "Failing to prepare is preparing to fail". The more setting up and planning you can do in the unstressed environment of your home, the more laid back will be your voyage.

The Dashboard

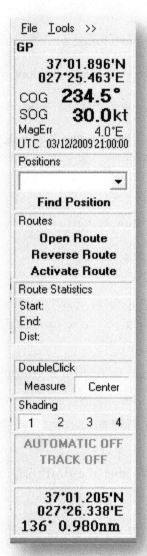

Top Menu
GPS Status. (Red in DR Mode)
Latitude
Longitude
True Course Over Ground
Speed Over Ground
Computed Magnetic Variation
UTC Time
Position database access

Find Position
Routes quick access
Open Route
Reverse Route
Activate Route
Loaded route statistics
Start Waypoint
End Waypoint
Total Distance

Select Measure or Center

Select shading level.
Toggle Automatic mode On/Off
Toggle Tracking On/Off.

Position of Cursor
Bearing to Cursor
Distance to Cursor

Note: The dashboard shown is the default dashboard when SeaClear is installed. The dashboard display changes to accommodate instruments or transducers you may configure.

Plan and Create Routes
Tutorial Create a Complex Route

In this tutorial you will create a complex route to use for safe passage through islands and shallows to a safe harbour.

1. Open SeaClear

2. Select **Tools** / **Route Editor**

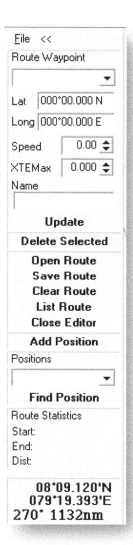

3. Reposition your chart display to show a complex navigation area.

4. Double click the locations for the waypoints for the route

5. If you find a waypoint is inserted instead of added to the route Right click on the waypoint and select **Delete**.

6. Right click on the charts and select **Extend**.

Now when you try to create a waypoint near the end of the route the route is extended correctly.

7. Click **Save** to save your route. Give the route a name and click **Save**.

8. Click **List** and your route displays as a form.

9. Give your way points meaningful names.

10. Click **Update** to save your changes to SeaClear but not to file

11. Click **Save Route** and your changes are saved

12. Click **Close Route**.

13. Click **Close Editor** to close the Route Editor.

Create Positions from a Route
Tutorial: Create Positions from a Route

With SeaClear. the way points you created are reusable as positions for creating new routes.

1. Open SeaClear

2. Select **File** / **Open Positions** and select a *route*. you have already saved. They are found in the **Routes** folder.

3. The positions plot on the chart and are listed with their names displayed.

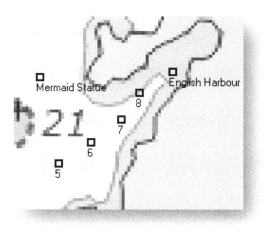

4. Select **File** / **Positions** / **Save As**.

5. When prompted, give your positions file a meaningful name and click **Save**.

6. The positions file is saved in the **waypts** folder.

Create a Route from Positions
Tutorial Create a Route from Positions

1. Open SeaClear.

2. Select **Files**/**Positions** /**Open**

3. Positions display on the chart with their names

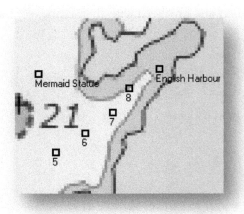

4. Select **Tools** / **Route Editor**.

5. The positions names display in the **Positions** dropdown box.

6. Select the first position for your route

7. Click **Add Position** and the position is converted to a way point for your route.

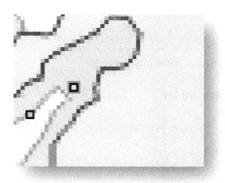

8. Select the second position for your route.

9. Click **Add Position** and the position is converted to a way point for your route.

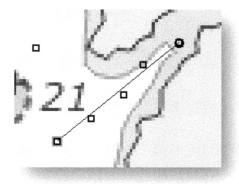

10. You can extend this new route by double clicking a distance from the second waypoint.

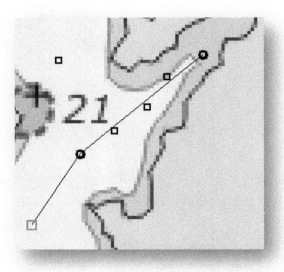

11. Click **Save** and give this new route a meaningful name.

12. Your route is saved in the **Routes** folder

Creating a Race Course

As a sailboat race can be regarded as an assessment of the skills of its' crew, the course is ideally set so the boats have to sail a beat, a reach and a run. A triangular course is the best for this and would be marked out by a number of buoys. This is the standard Olympic Course. The course starts from an imaginary line drawn from a 'committee boat' to the designated 'starting' buoy which are positioned to be perpendicular to the direction of the wind. This may cause delays in starting the race if the wind shifts direction causing the starting line to be re-positioned. The first leg of the race is towards the windward marker or buoy. Warning signals by means of both sound and vision are given telling the crews exactly how long until the race starts. The aim of each crew is to cross the start line at full speed exactly as the race starts. After rounding the windward mark the sailboats bear away onto a downwind leg to a second jibe marker. Next another jibe on a second downwind leg to the last mark which is called the 'downwind mark' (or 'leeward mark'). At this mark the boats turn into the wind once again to tack to the finish line.

Local conditions may make such a course undesirable or impossible and any configuration may be used, particularly so if laying buoys is impractical and natural or navigation marks are used. Some sailing clubs hold races on tidal stretches of rivers, and the strength of the flood and ebb tides can force the start line to even be approached downwind, whilst the course has to follow the meanderings of the river. Another common course uses just a windward and downwind leg.

Once created the racing course can be used in a number of ways.

- Printed out for display on a club's Race Notice Board

- Distributed to race participants in web site or via email.

- The race course can be easily amended to take in to account considerations such as wind shift, right up until near the start of the race.

- If a race has to be abandoned early participants normally report their GPS positions. These can be plotted on the chart to determine the race leader at the time (handicapping would have to be taken into account)

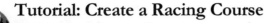

Tutorial: Create a Racing Course

In this tutorial you will create a general purpose race course for your sailing club. Each leg of the course is different, and tests reaching beating and running. The course can easily be adapted to suite differing wind conditions .

1. Decide the best position for your start line which consists of the committee boat and a start buoy.

2. Open SeaClear and right click where you want to position the committee boat. Select **Positions** / **Add.**

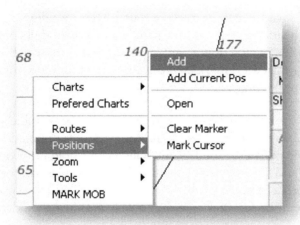

3. At the **Edit Positions** window give the position a meaningful name and click **Save**.

4. The created position displays on the chart with its name.

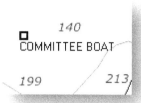

5. Repeat this procedure for the start buoy, reach buoy (they are on a reach to round this buoy) and the upwind buoy (they have to tack to get to, and round this buoy)

6. Select **File / Positions / Save As.**

7. When prompted give the race course a meaningful name and click **Save**. .

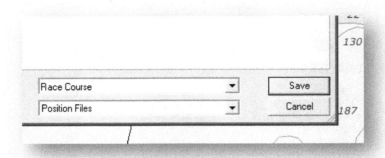

8. On, or before race day, print and post the chart with its positions on the race notice board and or send the course by email to the competitors. Send as an attachment the name race course file found in the **waypts** folder.

9. Alternatively post the race course on your sailing club's web site.

10. On future occasions the course can be modified by selecting **File** / **Positions** / **Unlock**.

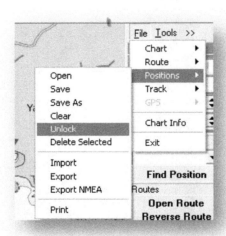

11. Position can now be moved by selecting and dragging

Setting up a Fuel Meter

SeaClear has the ability to display the amount of fuel you have used whilst motoring or motor-sailing. This gives you time to refuel when your tanks are down to set level.

Tutorial: Setting up a Fuel Consumption Meter.

In this tutorial you will set up a fuel meter in SeaClear to display a running total of fuel used.

1. Estimate the fuel consumption of your vessel (in litres) under the following conditions:

   - 0 kt (Idle)
   - 5.0 kt
   - 8.0 kt

   - 14.0 kt
   - 18.0 kt
   - 25.0 kt

2. With SeaClear closed, open the **SeaClear_2 Configurations Settings** file in a text editor. **Note** the file is stored in the same folder as SeaClear_2 exe file.

3. For each speed and consumption figure multiply each by 10.

4. At the [Fuel Data] section enter the fuel data as below:

```
[Fuel Data]

000=20
050=45
080=50
140=225
180=350
250=650
```

For example if your boats fuel consumption is as follow:

2.8 l/h @ 0.0Kt (Idle)   22.5 l/h @ 14.0Kt

4.5 l/h @ 5.0Kt   35.0 l/h @ 18.0Kt

8.0 l/h @ 8.0Kt   65.0 l.h @ 25.0Kt

Enter the following in [Fuel Data] section.

000=28   140=225

050=45   180=350

080=80   250=650

5. Save the file (ensure you do not change the file name and save as text.

6. Open SeaClear and turn **Automatic On**.

7. Fuel consumption displays at the Trip Panel of the Dashboard.

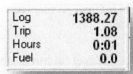

8. Fuel consumption is only estimated when **Engine On** is selected by right clicking on the panel.

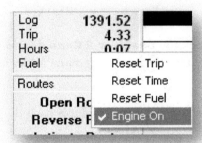

9. When you refuel, the fuel consumed data is zeroed by right clicking on the panel and selecting **Reset Fuel.**

Navigating
The Dashboard

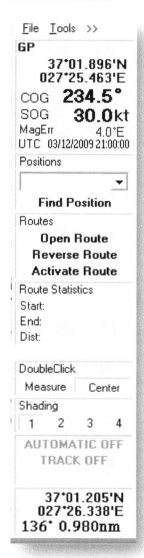

Top Menu
GPS Status. (Red in DR Mode)
Latitude
Longitude
True Course Over Ground
Speed Over Ground
Computed Magnetic Variation
UTC Time
Position database access

Find Position
Routes quick access
Open Route
Reverse Route
Activate Route
Loaded route statistics
Start Waypoint
End Waypoint
Total Distance

Select Measure or Center

Select shading level.
Toggle Automatic mode On/Off
Toggle Tracking On/Off.

Position of Cursor
Bearing to Cursor
Distance to Cursor

Note: The dashboard shown is the default dashboard when SeaClear is installed. The dashboard display changes to accommodate instruments or transducers you may configure.

Tutorial:Plot Your Position

1. With a correctly connected GPS your vessel's position is plotted on the chart and displayed in a dashboard panel.

2. Click **Automatic Off** to toggle whether the display follows the vessel's position on screen.

3. Press **Ctrl + Z** or **X** to zoom the display in or out.

4. With **Automatic Off** and **Centre** selected double clicking the chart centres your vessel on the screen

5. Clicking and holding down the left mouse button allows you the drag and pan the chart.

6. With **Automatic On** and **Measure** selected double clicking and holding the left mouse button allows you the measure a distance on the chart. The bottom dashboard panel turns green and displays position in Lat and Long of first point clicked and the bearing and length of the distance you are measuring..

```
37°01.857'N
027°25.314'E
199° 0.006nm
```

7. **Clicking Track On /Track Off** toggles the creation and display of a track of your route.

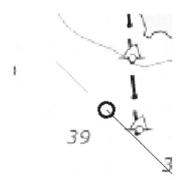

8. With GPS off or disconnected the top dashboard panel turns red to indicate dead reckoning mode. You can adjust course and speed via the **Course** and **Speed** data panels.

Tutorial Track Your Course

1. Tracking characteristics are setup in the **Log +Track** tab of the **SeaClear Setup** window accessed via **Tools / Properties.**

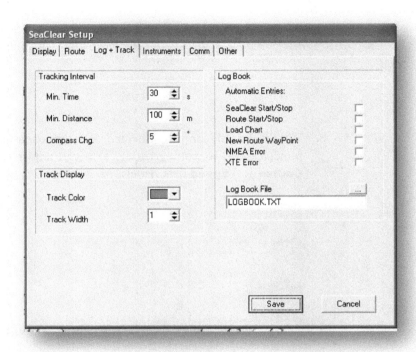

2. Tracking is toggled on and of by selection **Track On** or **Track Off**

3. The track is automatically saved in the **Traces** folder with the file name of the current date. A new track file is automatically created at 00.00 every day.

4. With **Tracking Off** , open the **Traces** folder and rename the current track file to **old.trc**.

5. When tracking is started again by selection **Track On** or **Track Off** a new track file is created with the current date as file name..

The Navigation Dashboard (Route Active)

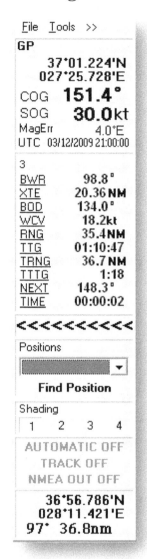

Next Waypoint number
BWR: Bearing to waypoint,
XTE: Crosstrack error,
BOD: Bearing from Origin to Dest
WCV: Waypoint Closure Velocity
RNG: Range to waypoint,
TTG: Time to go to waypoint,
TRNG: Range to go end of route,
TTTG: Time to go from current
position using waypoint speed data.
NEXT: Next bearing is shown.
TIME

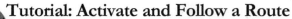

Tutorial: Activate and Follow a Route

1. Open a route by selecting **File**/ **Route** / **Open**.

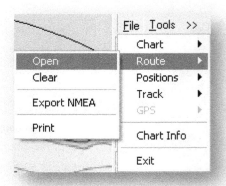

2. Activate a route by right clicking on the chart and selecting **Route** / **Activate Route.**

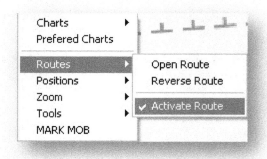

3. Route data displays in the dashboard.

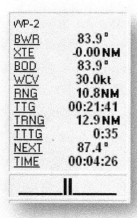

4. Select **NMEA OUT OFF** to pass data to your auto pilot

5. To reverse right click on the chart and select **Routes** / **Reverse Route**.

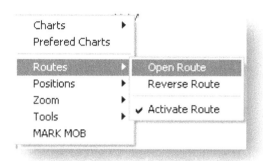

MOB (Man Over Board

A crucial safety feature of SeaClear is MOB. Pressing **Ctrl** + **Space** marks your vessel's current position with a MOB marker, and displays Lat and Long of the victims position as well as bearing and distance.

Tutorial MOB Man Over Board

In this tutorial you will practice, man overboard prodedures to quickly recover the victim when time in the water may be critical.

1. Open SeaClear

1. When the victim falls overboard press CTRL + SPACE.

2. A MOB marker is placed at the vessels position

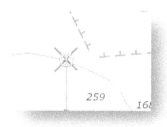

3. The data panel at the bottom of the dashboard turns cyan and displays **Lat Long Bearing** and **Distance** to the MOB.

```
36°57.937'N
027°38.952'E
0°  0.175nm
```

4. Turn your vessel to the bearing indicated in the panel, and you are directed to the last known position of the MOB.

Note: Keep a good lookout and do not run over your MOB

5. To cancel MOB right click on the MOB marker and select **Positions** / **Clear Marker**.

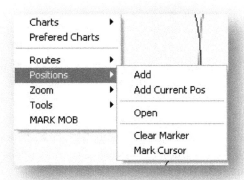

Printing Charts

It is always useful to have onboard hard copy paper charts to refer to when your electronics lets you down.

Tutorial: Printing a Chart.

In this tutorial you will print a chart and include such details as Route Positions and Tracks

1. Open SeaClear

2. Position the view of chart you wish to print.

3. Load any Positions or Route you wish to print with the chart.

4. Select **File** / **Chart** / **Print Chart**

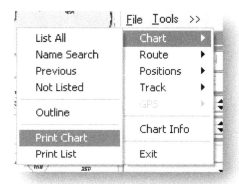

5. At the **Print Chart** window select the items you want printed and whether to print the screen view or the complete chart.

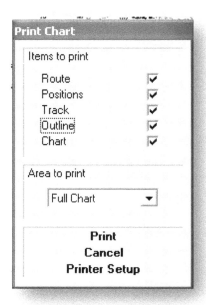

6. Click **Printer Setup** and at the **Print** window select the printer from the **Name** dropdown box.

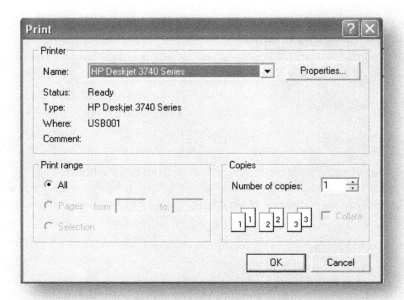

7. Click **OK** and at the **Print Chart** window click **Print.** Your chart is printed at your selected printer

Making SeaClear Portable

There may be occasions where you would like to plan your sailing trip on your home computer and then transfer all the details and maps to your on board lap top. The advent of cheap USB memory stick drives means this is an easy process.

Tutorial: Setting up SeaClear to run on a USB Memory Stick.

In this tutorial you will set up SeaClear to: run from a USB memory stick on your home PC, .load charts you need, and then transfer the complete installation including the charts to your on board PC.

1. Insert your USB memory stick in a free USB port.

2. Windows detects the USB Memory stick and assigns it a Drive Letter. Click the Windows **Start** button and select **My Computer** Make a careful note of the assigned drive letter

3. Install SeaClear to your USB memory stick as you would to a hard drive.

4. Run MapCal from the USB memory stick and load any charts you have to the **SeaClear/Charts** directory on the USB memory stick.

5. Run SeaClear from the USB memory stick and check that the map has been loaded. By selecting **File / Chart / List All**.

6. Remove the memory stick from your home PC and plug it into your on board PC. Windows assigns a drive letter to the memory stick. This drive letter may not match the drive letter assigned to the memory stick on your home PC. If the drive letters do mot match continue from step 7. If the drive letters do match jump to step 14.

7. This step is important as you have to assign a drive letter to your plugged in USB memory stick that matches the drive letter when plugged in to your home PC.

8. On your onboard PC Select **Start** and right click on **My Computer** and select **Manage**.

9. At the **Disk Management** window click **Disk Management** at the bottom of the right-hand pane.

10. The USB memory stick is listed as a drive

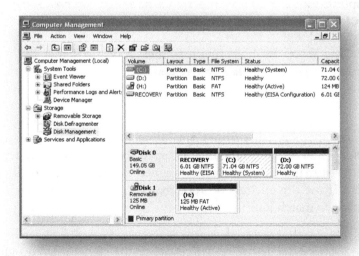

11. Right click on this pane and select **Change Drive Letter and Paths**

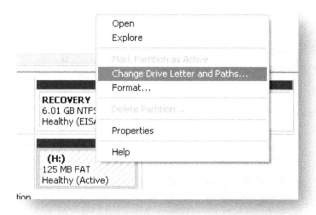

12. At the **Change Drive Letter and Paths For ?:** window click **Change** and select a drive letter from the drop down list. The drive letter you select must match the drive letter assigned on your home PC.

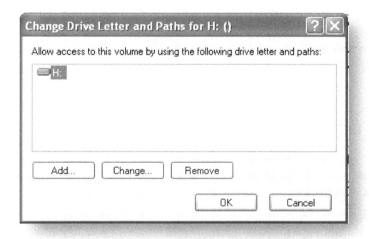

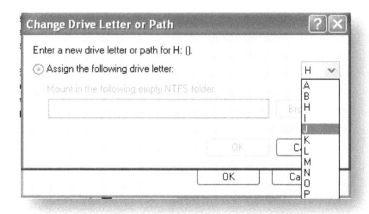

13. At the **Confirm** window click **Yes**.

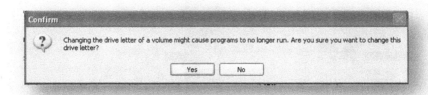

14. Click **OK** and the new drive letter is assigned to your onboard USB memory stick.

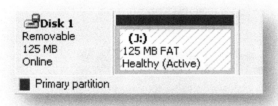

15. Close the open windows and run SeaClear from the USB memory stick by double clicking the **SeaClear_2** icon.

16. SeaClear will run as it did on your home PC with the same charts, routes, positions and tracks.

17. When finished with your on board PC you can transfer the complete installation for use on your home PC by repeating steps 6 to 14.

Running SeaClear under Linux

Tutorial: Running SeaClear under the Linux Operating System

1. From within Linux open FireFox or another Linux compatible browser

2. Navigate to the Sping.com page and click on **SeaClear II Full install sc_setup.exe**

3. When prompted by the **Opening sc_setup.exe** window select **Open with** Ensure the path **usr/bin/wine (default)** displays in the dropdown box and click **OK**.

4. Your are prompted with a **Setup** window with the message This will install SeaClear. Do you wish to continue? Click **Yes**

5. When prompted by further windows click **Next**, **Install OK** or **Finish** and SeaClear is installed on your Linux machine.

6. If your GPS connects through serial COM, you must only remember that in Linux, COM1=/dev/ttyS0, COM2=/dev/ttyS1, etc.

7. After connecting the GPS, run "dmesg" from the Terminal application in Linux to find out: where your GPS is connected. You should see lines like these:

**[23802.383672] pl2303 2-1:1.0: pl2303 converter detected
[23802.450819] usb 2-1: pl2303 converter now attached to ttyUSB2**

8. The problem is SeaClear doesn't recognize "/dev/...", so we can get around the problem making a "sym link" from "COM to USB". I chose COM1 as this is the default com port for SeaClear to avoid interference with other things In the Terminal application type:

sudo ln -sb /dev/ttyUSB2 /dev/ttyS0

Note: Remember Linux is case sensitive

9. From Wine run SeaClear and check for connection via Tools System Input Monitor.

4. Integrating SeaClear

Note: SeaClear can open a maximum of 3 COM Ports (One Rx/Tx, two Rx) If you need to connect more than 3 transducers you have to use a NMEA Multiplexer that takes multiple NMEA inputs and outputs a single NMEA data stream

GPS (Global Positioning System)

Why do I need GPS?

The **Global Positioning System** (**GPS**) is a U.S. space-based global navigation satellite system. It provides reliable positioning, navigation, and timing services to worldwide users on a continuous basis in all weather, day and night, anywhere on or near the Earth which has an unobstructed view of four or more GPS satellites.

GPS is made up of three segments: Space, Control and User:

The Space Segment is composed of 24 to 32 satellites in Medium Earth Orbit and also includes the boosters required to launch them into orbit.

The Control Segment is composed of a Master Control Station, an Alternate Master Control Station, and a host of dedicated and shared Ground Antennas and Monitor Stations.

The User Segment is composed of hundreds of thousands of U.S. and allied military users of the secure GPS Precise Positioning Service, and tens of millions of civil, commercial and scientific users of the Standard Positioning Service. GPS satellites broadcast signals from space that GPS receivers use to provide three-dimensional location (latitude, longitude, and altitude) plus precise time.

GPS has become a widely used aid to navigation worldwide, and a useful tool for map-making, land surveying, commerce, scientific uses, tracking and surveillance, and hobbies such as geocaching and waymarking. Also, the precise time reference is used in many applications including the scientific study of earthquakes and as a time synchronization source for cellular network protocols.

GPS has become a mainstay of transportation systems worldwide, providing navigation for aviation, ground, and maritime operations. Disaster relief and emergency services depend upon GPS for location and timing capabilities in their life-saving missions. The accurate timing that GPS provides facilitates everyday activities such as banking, mobile phone operations, and even the control of power grids. Farmers, surveyors, geologists and countless others perform their work more efficiently, safely, economically, and accurately using the free and open GPS signals.

For many yachtsmen GPS has become a "must have" rather than "nice to have" whether that be a standalone unit, or one that integrates with a chart plotter and navigation system such as SeaClear.

A GPS will only give an accurate vessel position course and speed if:

Your GPS has been correctly fitted and connected to SeaClear.

You have set SeaClear to match the datum used by the GPS. If the GPS and SeaClear settings do not match, your plotted position on the chart can be as much a 1000m out.

Note: A GPS should not be seen as an alternative to the use of paper charts *and* manual navigation techniques

Which GPS Do I Need?

Your may already own a suitable GPS. It may be one of the main types below:

Standalone GPS with screen. This has the flexibility to be used independently from SeaClear but may need a separate power supply provided by batteries.

Your existing chartplotter may have integrated GPS. It may have a data output connector to connect to your PC.

Mouse or puck style GPS with USB interface, hardwired or Bluetooth. The hardwired versions are supplied with power via the USB port.
Most Bluetooth versions can be plugged into a USB port to recharge their internal batteries.

 Whichever GPS you choose, it must be capable of connecting to a PC, and outputting data in the form of NMEA sentences. The connection could be serial USB (both cabled) or Bluetooth (wireless). Many older GPS units do not have PC connection, or only output as proprietary data, not compatible with SeaClear.

Installing a GPS

Refer to the documentation supplied with your GPS. Pay particular attention to a reliable power supply, and site the GPS where it can see clear sky and is sited away from other sensitive electronic devices.

If the GPS has a serial output, and your computer does not have serial inputs, you will have to purchase a "serial to USB" adaptor cable. If you need such a cable you have to install the correct driver, supplied by the cable manufacturer, to set up a virtual serial port. If the GPS is Bluetooth, pair it with your PC by following the manufacturer's documentation and a COM port is automatically created.

Tutorial: Connecting GPS to SeaClear

In this tutorial you will set up SeaClear with GPS to accurately plot your position, speed and course.

1. From the **Tools** menu select **Properties** to open the **SeaClear Setup** window.

2. Select the **Comm.** tab.

3. As communication with a GPS receiver may be two way, select **TX/RX 1** in the **NMEA Connection** area of the window.

4. Set the **PC Port Com** to match the COM port your GPS unit is using to communicate with your PC. This could be a physical serial port or a virtual serial port. To help you identify the correct serial port, you can use a utility such as **SOB Ports**.

5. Set the **BPS** (Bits per second) to **4800** (the default speed for GPS

6. In the **GPS Datum Setting** area set the datum to match the datum your GPS is using. (Refer to the manufacturers documentation) It is important that the datum set in SeaClear matches the GPS datum, otherwise your plotted position will not be accurate. Most modern GPSs use **WGS84**.

7. Click **Save** to save your settings and return to the main **SeaClear** window.

8. Check the setup is ok by selecting **Tools, System, NMEA Input Monitor**, The **NMEA Input Monitor** window the NMEA sentences displayed should include sentences starting with: **$G** ,

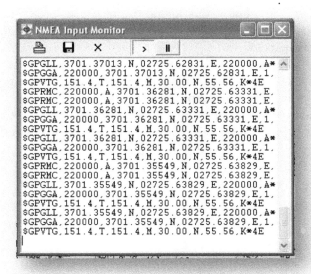

9. Your position displays in the dashboard.

10. Your vessel is plotted on the chart.

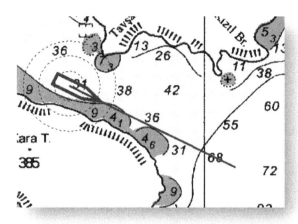

Note: If your position is not displayed in the dashboard, or on the chart ensure your GPS is set to output NMEA. If you have set your GPS to its simulator mode, your position may not be displayed or plotted. In simulator mode some GPS units do not output a position fix message which is needed by SeaClear to ensure reliability of the data.

AIS
Why do I need AIS
Error! Bookmark not defined.? (Automatic Identification System.)

There are situations during poor visibility or darkness when the display of other vessels position, course and speed will increase safety. A radar system will plot other vessels position but not their course and speed. Radar cannot see over the horizon or behind headlands and is a costly system outside many yachtsmen's budget. An AIS system is a low cost system (from 150$) of displaying essential information from other vessels, within VHF range, to minimise the risk of collisions.

AIS gives information of all the ships in your area, their speed and courses and how to contact them (name, call sign, MMSI). This information is publically broadcast on VHF radio which can be picked up either by other ships or by shore based receivers.

AIS works best over a range of a few miles as the AIS signal is more or less limited to line of sight to the horizon (usually 10-20 miles).

All commercial vessels (over 300 T or passenger carriers)are required to have a working Class A AIS transponder (Transmitter and Receiver) on board that transmits vessel information and receives AIS from other vessels in VHF range.

It is likely that AIS will replace Navtex over the next few years. Shore based AIS stations have the capability to create virtual navigation aids without having to install the physical navigation aids themselves.

For the recreational yachtsman there are a number of Class B transponders (Transmitter and Receiver) on the market that transmit more limited data but still receive and display full data from other vessels'.

Low cost B Class AIS receivers are the entry level for yachtsmen to receive all AIS information from other vessels.

AIS comes into its own in congested waterways with perhaps limited visibility. It is reassuring to have the position, course etc of other vessels displayed along with your own position on an electronic chart.

AIS has now been added to several personal SART (Search and Rescue Transmitters)

SeaClear connected to an AIS unit continuously computes your own course and the course of other vessels within VHF range and warns you visually and audibly if a collision is a risk. This allows you to take early evasive action even if you cannot see the vessel(s) in question.

AIS information is transmitted in NEMA sentences similar to the data output from GPS units which include:

- MMSI number of vessel - vessel's unique identification
- Navigation status - e.g. at anchor, under way using engine, not under command etc
- Rate of turn - right or left, 0 to 720 degrees per minute
- Speed over ground - 0.1 knot resolution from 0 to 102 knots
- Longitude - to 1/10000 minute and Latitude - to 1/10000 minute
- Course over ground - relative to true north to 0.1 degree
- True Heading - 0 to 359 degrees from a gyrocompass
- Time stamp - UTC time accurate to nearest second.
- In addition, the following data is broadcast every 6 minutes:

- MMSI number - vessel's unique identification
- IMO number - this number always remains with the ship
- Radio call sign - international radio call sign assigned to vessel
- Name - Name of vessel
- Type of ship/cargo
- Dimensions of ship - to nearest meter
- Location of positioning system's (e.g. GPS) antenna onboard the vessel
- Type of positioning system - usually GPS or DGPS
- Draught of ship - 0.1 meter to 25.5 meters
- Destination - max 20 characters

ETA at destination - UTC month/date hour: minute

 AIS will only give you an accurate and reliable indication of another vessel(s) position, speed and course etc if:

The other vessel has an AIS transponder fitted

Your AIS unit has been correctly fitted and connected to SeaClear.

You are within VHF reception range of the other vessel(s).

The other vessel(s) transponder is operating correctly.

AIS should not be seen as an alternative to keeping a good lookout.

Which AIS do I Need?

It is possible to connect to the output from a general purpose VHF receiver. The receiver must be able to receive Marine Channels 87B and 88B and have a discriminator output. Most receivers do not have this output but it may be possible to modify the circuit board to create this output. In addition you need software such as Shipplotter that decodes the discriminator output and produces NMEA for use with SeaClear.

Type A AIS transponders are normally limited to commercial vessels. AIS data is received and transmitted but outside the scope of most yachtsmen..

Type B AIS transponders transmit limited AIS data but still receive full AIS information from other vessels. Again outside the scope of most yachtsmen

Type B receivers are more popular with recreational yachtsmen being of relatively low cost and easy to fit. They receive all AIS information.

Do I need a one or two channel AIS receiver?

To reduce bandwidth AIS transponders transmit on two alternate VHF channels (87B and 88B) Type B *receivers* are available in single or two channel versions. A single channel receiver will still receive all AIS data but it may take fractionally longer to receive full messages.

Installing AIS (Automatic Identification System.)

Refer to the documentation supplied with your AIS unit. Pay particular attention to a reliable power supply, and site the VHF aerial as high as possible to ensure maximum VHF reception. You can use a VHF Splitter to share an existing VHF aerial.

If the AIS unit has a serial output, and your computer does not have serial inputs, you will have to purchase a "serial to USB" adaptor cable. If you need such a cable you have to install the correct driver, supplied by the cable manufacturer, to set up a virtual serial port on your computer

Tutorial: Connecting AIS to SeaClear

In this tutorial you will set up SeaClear to display AIS data and enable alarms for potential collision scenarios.

1. From the **Tools** menu select **Properties** to open the **SeaClear Setup** window.

2. Select the **Comm.** tab.

3. As communication with an AIS receiver is *input* only, select either **RX2** or **RX3** in the **NMEA Connection** area of the window.

4. Set the **PC Port Com** to match the COM port your AIS unit is using to communicate with your computer.

5. Set the **BPS** (Bits per second) to 38400 (the default speed for AIS)

6. Select the **Instruments** tab.

7. In the **AIS** area of the window ensure **Show AIS Targets**, **Show AIS Panel** and **Show Labels** are selected.

8. At the **CPA Max** (**C**losest **P**oint of **A**pproach) input box, enter 1 nm. The higher the value the more vessels will be identified by SeaClear as collision risks

9. At the **TCPA** (**T**ime to **C**losest **P**oint of **A**pproach) enter 5 mins. The higher the value the more vessels will be identified by SeaClear as collision risks

Note: The above suggested values for **CPA** and **TCPA** will trigger AIS warnings if under current conditions SeaClear predicts you will come within 1nm(**CPA**) of another AIS equipped vessel in less than 5 minutes. (**TCPA**)

10. Select blue as the **Target Color** and **Large** as the **Target Size.**

11. Click **Save** to save your settings and return to the main **SeaClear** window.

12. Check the setup is ok by selecting **Tools, System, NMEA Input Monitor,** The **NMEA Input Monitor** window the NMEA sentences displayed should include sentence starting with: **!AIVDM** ,

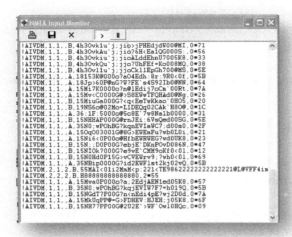

Tutorial: Using AIS Target Display

Use this tutorial to explore the display of AIS targets, the display of vessel's AIS information and the finding of a particular vessel on your screen.

1. Vessels equipped with AIS transponders and within VHF range, are displayed on the chart as AIS targets.

Note: Underway vessel's AIS targets are displayed with their name and a vector that indicates **HDT** (**H**ea**d**ing **T**rue) if available or **COG** (**C**ourse **O**ver **G**round)

2. Identified vessels are listed in the **AIS** drop down list. This is updated every time it is opened.

3. Select a vessel from the drop down list and click **Info** to open an **AIS Target Info** window which displays AIS data for the selected vessel.

4. Close the **AIS Target Info** window then click **Find** to centre the chart on the selected vessel.

Note: A selected AIS target is identified on the chart with a dotted rectangle.

5. Manually centre any AIS target on the chart and zoom in using Ctrl + Z or the mouse wheel to zoom to the maximum view of the target vessel. If the vessels dimensions have been correctly sent by the vessels transponder the vessel is displayed "to scale" on the chart.

6. Locate another AIS target and right mouse click on it, then select **Tools AIS Info** to open the **AIS Target Info** window

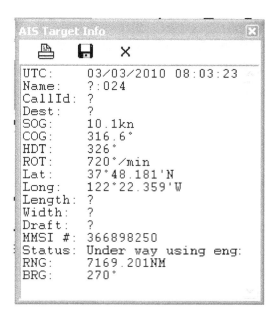

```
AIS Target Info                    ⊠
    🖨    💾    ✕
UTC:      03/03/2010 08:03:23
Name:     ?:024
CallId:   ?
Dest:     ?
SOG:      10.1kn
COG:      316.6°
HDT:      326°
ROT:      720°/min
Lat:      37°48.181'N
Long:     122°22.359'W
Length:   ?
Width:    ?
Draft:    ?
MMSI #:   366898250
Status:   Under way using eng:
RNG:      7169.201NM
BRG:      270°
```

Note: You can monitor any AIS target by keeping this window open. The information is updated continuously. This vessel is shown turning to starboard as shown in the **ROT** area of the window. (A negative-**ROT** indicates a turn to Port)

7. Return to the chart and you can see the vessel turning as indicated by the vector line from the vessel

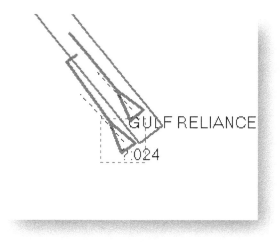

8.   AIS base stations are identified on the chart as below

9.   Right mouse click on the base station target, then select **Tools AIS Info** to open the **AIS Target Info** window

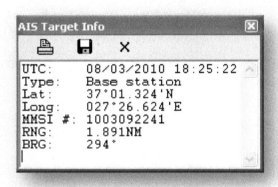

Tutorial: Simulate a Collision Risk

In this tutorial you will simulate a collision risk so you can experience AIS warnings. You can practice collision avoidance, before it happens in a live situation.

1. Switch off your GPS so that SeaClear reverts to its **DR** (**D**ead **R**eckoning) state as indicated in the **DR** window.

2. Manually reposition chart to show the AIS target of a vessel underway.

3. Reposition your vessel near to the AIS target by right mouse clicking close to the AIS target and select **Tools**, **DR Pos**. Your vessel displays on the chart at the selected position.

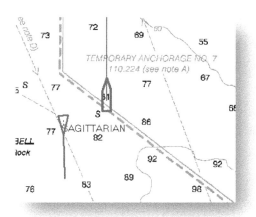

4. In the **DR** window adjust **Course** and **Speed** to create a collision risk with your chosen AIS target.

5. A collision warning displays on the chart. The display shows the target vessel with a CPA ring equal to the target vessel's length, In addition, your vessel display a ring set at the CPA you have already set.(Not shown in this diagram)

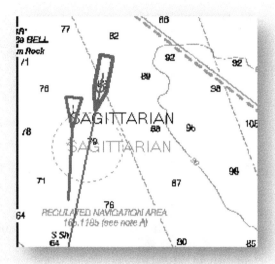

6. Right click on the target vessel and select **Tools AIS Info** and the AIS **Target AIS Info** windows opens for the target vessel which also displays the **CPA** and **TCPA**

7. You can use this information to hail the other vessel or take evasive action. If you take evasive action (In this case adjust your **DR** settings) and the collision risk is removed the collision warning is removed from the screen and **CPA** and **TCPA** are removed from the **AIS Target Info** window

Note: Taking evasive action will remove the risk of collision with this vessel but may create a collision risk with other vessels. Zooming out may reveal other collision warnings on the chart.

Using Shore Based AIS
Why do I need a Shore Based AIS

You may be a harbourmaster, marina manager or yacht club commodore where it would be useful, or even essential to be alerted when an AIS equipped vessel approaches or enters your harbour/marina. With a wind transducer connected you can relay current local wind conditions to any approaching vessel as well as berthing details or which pontoon to use.

Tutorial Setting up Shore based AIS

In this tutorial you will set up shore based AIS . If you have a Type B receiver you can monitor vessel in your area or immediate harbour. Before setting up a shore based ensure any GPS you have is is not connected

1. From the **Tools** menu select **Properties** to open the SeaClear Setup window.

2. Select **Shape** as **Circle** . Color as **Yellow** and **Size** as **Huge**. This allows your shore based AIS to be easily distinguished from AIS *vessel* targets.

3. Click **Save** to save your settings.

4. Centre a chart to display the location of your proposed shore based AIS. This may be your harbour office, marina office, yacht club or even your home.

5. Right click on this location and select **Tools**, **DR Pos.** Your shore based AIS is displayed at this location

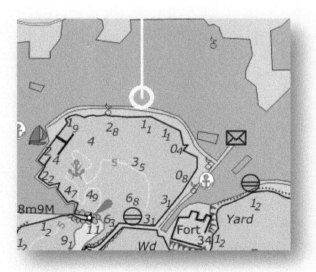

6. Connect your AIS as shown above on page 79.

7. Approaching vessels display on the chart

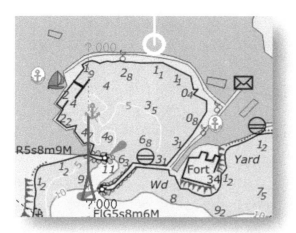

8. Vessels in harbour display on the chart.

9. If you set **Radar Rings** to **2** in the **SeaClear Setup** window they display on the chart allowing you to visually access "distance off" for detected AIS equipped vessels. Here is vessel ISLA TWO approaching the outer ring.

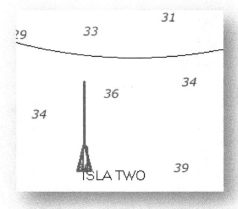

10. Here is vessel ISLA TWO passing the outer ring.

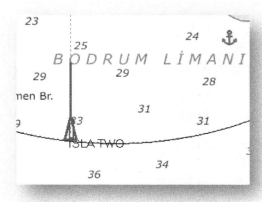

11. You can set your shore based AIS **CPA** to match your Radar Rings. Approaching vessels trigger a collision risk warning. Here is ISLA TWO approaching with the warning activated.

12. Information about the vessel is displayed by right clicking and selecting **Tools AIS Info**

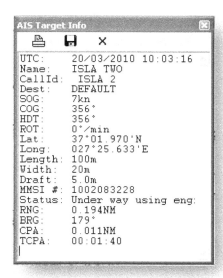

13. This information which includes **Callid**, **Length**, **Width** and **Draft** is essential to a harbourmaster to decide on a suitable berth.

SART (Search and Rescue Transmitter)
Why do I need SART?

AIS has now been added to several personal SART (**Se**arch and **R**escue **T**ransmitters) beacons. All chartplotters, or PC's, equipped with an AIS-receiver will receive the messages from the SART beacon.

The SART sends an AIS message type 1 which contains the position information and an AIS message type 14 which is a broadcast alert message with a "pre defined" text, which will be "AIS SART ACTIVE"

Currently, an activated AIS equipped SART appears as a ship icon with an additional message "AIS SART active.

Each plotter, which can receive and display AIS data, can also receive and display data from the AIS equipped SART. Although this type of SART has a maximum VHF range of about 3 nm, from a vessel, they are particularly useful in a MOB (**M**an **O**ver**B**oard) situation plotting the victim's position range and bearing. The USCG have carried out tests with AIS SART beacons and achieved reception ranges of up to 132 nm It is likely a space based AIS system will be implemented soon which will allow unlimited range to the SART signal.

Which SART do I need?

There are now several personal SART beacons on the market. Some are automatically triggered when immersed other need manual activation. They are all classed as Type B transmitters. The price point may be the determining factor when choosing a personal SART beacon. You main requirement is the AIS feature.

Installing a SART.

As personal SART beacons are essentially portable they need no installation but only have a lifespan of about 48 months. This ensures the internal batteries are fit for purpose.

Tutorial: Testing a SART with SeaClear.

All personal SART beacons have a test feature to ensure they are in working order. Refer to the manufacturer's documentation. When set in test mode an AIS message is transmitted.

1. Test your SART by putting into test mode within range of your AIS/SeaClear installation

2. The SART location is displayed on the chart as a vessel AIS target.

3. The AIS target in test mode depends on the AIS SART model

Note: The International Marine Organisation suggested the following words of the identification of the target:

- For the test mode, use the text .SART TEST..

- For the active SART, use the text .SART ACTIVE..

They suggested a possible alternative wording::

1st test message would use text .SART UNDER TEST.

Final test message would use text .SART TEST OVER..

Active message would use text .SART ACTIVE..

Depth Transducer
Why do I need a Depth Transducer

Depth information is transmitted in NEMA sentences similar to the data output from GPS units. This gives you an indication on screen of the depth below the transducer and warns you when the depth is below the Depth Alarm limit you have set.

SeaClear will only give you an accurate and reliable indication of depth, if:

Your depth transducer has been correctly fitted and connected to SeaClear.

You have correctly configured SeaClear to work with your depth transducer.

Note Depth information via SeaClear should not be seen as an alternative to keeping a good lookout and referring to paper charts.

Which Depth Transducer Do I Need?

"Thru hull" transducers pick up depth information from within the hull without the need for drilling holes. They are best suited to GRP hulls.

"In Hull" transducers are fitted by drilling a hole in the hull so that the transducer is in contact with the water. They are harder to fit and may become fouled.

"Transom mounted" transducers are mounted totally outside the hull normally at the transom. Installation is easy but the transducer is exposed to a risk of damage and fouling.

Some depth transducers send NMEA without the need for a depth display instrument

Installing a Depth Transducer

Refer to the documentation supplied with your depth transducer.

If the transducer has a serial output, and your computer does not have serial inputs, you will have to purchase a "serial to USB" adaptor cable. If you need such a cable you have to install the correct driver, supplied by the cable manufacturer, to set up a virtual serial port on your computer. The output may be connected directly from the transducer or via any depth instrument attached. The depth output must be in NMEA.

Tutorial: Connecting a Depth Transducer to SeaClear

In this tutorial you will set up SeaClear to display AIS data and enable alarms for potential run aground scenarios.

1. From the **Tools** menu select **Properties** to open the **SeaClear Setup** window.

2. Select the **Comm** tab.

3. As communication with a depth transducer is *receive* only, select either **RX2** or **RX3** in the **NMEA Connection** area of the window.

4. Set the **PC Port Com** to match the COM port your depth transducer is using to communicate with your computer.

5. Set the **BPS** (**B**its **p**er **s**econd) to 4800.(The default speed for depth data)

6. Select the **Instruments** tab.

7. In the **Depth Display** area of the window select m (for metres) at the **Show Depth** input box

8. At the **Depth Alarm** input box, enter a depth alarm value at least 2 metres more than the draft of your vessel.

9. At the **Trans Depth** (Transponder Depth) select a value that matches how far below the surface your depth transponder is.

10. Click **Save** to save your settings.

11. Check the setup is ok by selecting **Tools, System, NMEA Input Monitor**, The **NMEA Input Monitor** window the NMEA sentences displayed should include a sentence starting with: **$SDDPT,** as in line 12 of the data shown below.

```
NMEA Input Monitor
$HEHDT,315.0,M*31
$GPRMC,120324.55,A,3701.19936,N,02726.04764,E,5.0,315.0,040310,
$WIMWV,17.1,R,18.1,N,A*2C
$VWVLW,0.051,N,0.051,N*4C
$HEHDT,315.0,M*31
$GPRMC,120325.55,A,3701.20034,N,02726.04641,E,5.0,315.0,040310,
$WIMWV,16.6,R,19.2,N,A*28
$VWVLW,0.054,N,0.054,N*4C
$HEHDT,315.0,M*31
$GPRMC,120326.56,A,3701.20132,N,02726.04518,E,5.0,315.0,040310,
$WIMWV,10.0,R,18.2,N,A*29
$SDDPT,11.1,2.0*64
$VWVLW,0.057,N,0.057,N*4C
$HEHDT,315.0,M*31
$GPRMC,120327.58,A,3701.20230,N,02726.04395,E,5.0,315.0,040310,
$WIMWV,18.5,R,18.5,N,A*23
$SDDPT,10.9,2.0*6D
$VWVLW,0.060,N,0.060,N*4C
$HEHDT,315.0,M*31
$GPRMC,120328.59,A,3701.20328,N,02726.04272,E,5.0,315.0,040310,
$WIMWV,8.3,R,19.7,N,A*17
$SDDPT,8.1,2.0*5C
$VWVLW,0.063,N,0.063,N*4C
$HEHDT,315.0,M*31
$GPRMC,120329.59,A,3701.20426,N,02726.04149,E,5.0,315.0,040310,
$WIMWV,11.5,R,18.2,N,A*2D
$GPRMC,120255.14,A,3701.17094,N,02726.08331,E,5.0,315.0,040310,
```

Note: A depth warning is triggered when the water depth below the transponder is less than the value you have set for the **Depth Alarm**.

Tutorial: Using Depth Display and Simulate a Depth Warning
Use this tutorial to explore the display of depths and depth warnings.

1. Depth data is displayed as shown

    Note: Depth data is displayed with **Automatic on** or **Automatic Off.**

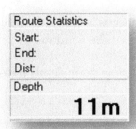

2. Simulate a depth warning by reducing the alarm settings and SeaClear displays a depth alarm.

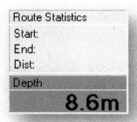

Note: Remember to reset the **Depth Alarm** setting to a sensible value or the warning will be triggered continuously.

Wind Transducer
Why do I need a Wind Transducer?

Wind strength and direction information is transmitted in NEMA sentences similar to the data output from GPS unit,

SeaClear will only give you an accurate and reliable indication of wind direction and speed if:

Your wind transducer has been correctly fitted and connected to SeaClear.

You have correctly configured SeaClear to work with your wind transducer.

Which Wind Transducer Do I Need?

Most wind systems consist of a masthead transducer and a wind display instrument

If you do not need a wind display instrument it is possible to buy just the masthead transducer that outputs data in NMEA

Installing Wind Transducer

Refer to the documentation supplied with your wind transducer. Pay particular attention to a reliable power supply, and site the unit as high as possible to ensure it is in "clear air".

If the wind transducer has a serial output, and your computer does not have serial inputs, you will have to purchase a "serial to USB" adaptor cable. If you need such a cable you have to install the correct driver, supplied by the cable manufacturer, to set up a virtual serial port on your computer

Tutorial: Connecting a Wind Transducer to SeaClear

In this tutorial you will set up SeaClear to display wind data on screen and on the chart.

1. From the **Tools** menu select **Properties** to open the **SeaClear Setup** window.

2. Select the **Comm** tab.

3. As communication with a wind transducer is receive only, select either **RX2** or **RX3** in the **NMEA Connection** area of the window.

4. Set the **PC Port Com** to match the COM port your wind transducer is using to communicate with your computer.

5. Set the **BPS** (Bits per second) to **4800**.

6. Select the **Instruments** tab.

7. In the **Wind Display** area of the window set the **Show Wind Data** to **kn**. (Knots)

8. Set the **Arrow Color** to red.

9. Click **Save** to save your settings and return to the main **SeaClear** window.

10. Check the setup is ok by selecting **Tools**, **System**, **NMEA Input Monitor**, The **NMEA Input Monitor** window the NMEA sentences displayed should include a sentence starting with: **$WIMWV,** as in line 3 of the data shown below.

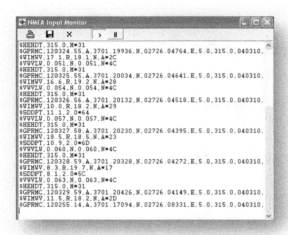

Tutorial: Using Wind Display

Use this tutorial to explore the display of wind information in SeaClear

1. Wind data is displayed on the screen the top line of the wind display shows the true wind direction as 22 degrees relative to the vessel with strength of 7.4 M/s. The second line shows an apparent wind direction as 17 degrees and a true wind direction of 337 degrees relative to the chart. The third line displays **VPW** (**V**elocity **P**arallel to **W**ind) Sometimes called 'velocity made good to windward'. If your destination were directly upwind your VMG and VPW would be the same.

Note: Apparent wind is the speed and relative direction from which the wind appears to blow with reference to a moving vessel.. It is the wind that yachts sail to.

Note: Wind data is only displayed on screen with **Automatic On**.

2. A wind arrow is also displayed on the chart at the vessel position which shows apparent wind direction.

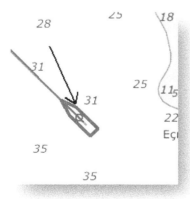

Note: The wind arrow is displayed on the chart with **Automatic On** or **Automatic Off**.

3. Differing wind strengths are indicated on the chart by the thickness and style of the wind arrow. Here the wind speed is **40kt**

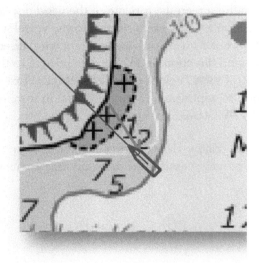 

Note: 0-2 kts it is dashed, 2-8 kts it is solid thin, 8-16 kts it is 2 pixel wide,   16-24 kts it is 3 pixel wide, over 24 kts fat 4 pixel wide arrow.

Fluxgate Compass
Why do I need a Fluxgate Compass

A basic fluxgate compass is a simple electromagnetic device that employs two or more small coils of wire around a core of highly permeable magnetic material, to directly sense the direction of the horizontal component of the earth's magnetic field. The advantages of this mechanism over a magnetic compass are that the reading is in electronic form and can be digitised and transmitted easily, displayed in SeaClear, and used by an electronic autopilot for course correction.

A fluxgate compass gives you an accurate Magnetic or True Heading. A GPS only displays COG. as degrees true The two values may differ as COG takes into account any effects on the vessel such as wind, current, leeway etc. In short the vessel points one way but goes another.

 A fluxgate compass will only give an accurate vessel heading if:

Your fluxgate compass has been correctly fitted and connected to SeaClear.

Any compass deviation has been assessed and allowed for.

Note: A fluxgate compass should not be seen as an alternative to a traditional magnetic compass and the use of paper charts *and* manual navigation techniques

Which Fluxgate Compass Do I Need?

There are many fluxgate compasses on the market, mainly designed for use with an autopilot. To use a fluxgate compass with SeaClear the output from the compass, or via the autopilot computer, must be NMEA.

Installing a Fluxgate Compass

Refer to the documentation supplied with your fluxgate compass. Pay particular attention to a reliable power supply, and site the compass as near as possible to the centreline of the vessel and away from sources of magnetic interference.

If the fluxgate compass, or the autopilot computer has a serial output, and your computer does not have serial inputs, you will have to purchase a "serial to USB" adaptor cable. If you need such a cable you have to install the correct driver, supplied by the cable manufacturer, to set up a virtual serial port on your computer

Tutorial: Connecting a Fluxgate Compass to SeaClear

In this tutorial you will set up SeaClear to display heading data

1. From the **Tools** menu select **Properties** to open the **SeaClear Setup** window.

2. Select the **Comm** tab.

3. As communication with a fluxgate compass is receive only, select either **RX2** or **RX3** in the **NMEA Connection** area of the window.

4. Set the **PC Port Com** to match the COM port your fluxgate compass is using to communicate with your computer.

5. Set the **BPS** (Bits per second) to 4800

6. Select the **Instruments** tab.

7. In the **Compass Display** area of the window ensure **Show Compass Data** is selected.

8. Click **Save** to save your settings and return to the main **SeaClear** window.

9. Check the setup is ok by selecting **Tools, System, NMEA Input Monitor**, The **NMEA Input Monitor** window the NMEA sentences displayed should include a sentence starting with: **$HEHDT,** as in line 1 of the data shown below.

```
NMEA Input Monitor                                    _ □ X
  🖨  🖫  ✕    >  ||
$HEHDT,315.0,M*31
$GPRMC,120324.55,A,3701.19936,N,02726.04764,E,5.0,315.0,040310,
$WIMWV,17.1,R,18.1,N,A*2C
$VWVLW,0.051,N,0.051,N*4C
$HEHDT,315.0,M*31
$GPRMC,120325.55,A,3701.20034,N,02726.04641,E,5.0,315.0,040310,
$WIMWV,16.6,R,19.2,N,A*28
$VWVLW,0.054,N,0.054,N*4C
$HEHDT,315.0,M*31
$GPRMC,120326.56,A,3701.20132,N,02726.04518,E,5.0,315.0,040310,
$WIMWV,10.0,R,18.2,N,A*29
$SDDPT,11.1,2.0*64
$VWVLW,0.057,N,0.057,N*4C
$HEHDT,315.0,M*31
$GPRMC,120327.58,A,3701.20230,N,02726.04395,E,5.0,315.0,040310,
$WIMWV,18.5,R,18.5,N,A*23
$SDDPT,10.9,2.0*6D
$VWVLW,0.060,N,0.060,N*4C
$HEHDT,315.0,M*31
$GPRMC,120328.59,A,3701.20328,N,02726.04272,E,5.0,315.0,040310,
$WIMWV,8.3,R,19.7,N,A*17
$SDDPT,8.1,2.0*5C
$VWVLW,0.063,N,0.063,N*4C
$HEHDT,315.0,M*31
$GPRMC,120329.59,A,3701.20426,N,02726.04149,E,5.0,315.0,040310,
$WIMWV,11.5,R,18.2,N,A*2D
$GPRMC,120255.14,A,3701.17094,N,02726.08331,E,5.0,315.0,040310,
```

Tutorial: Using Heading Display

Use this tutorial to explore the display the compass heading of your vessel on screen.

1. The **Compass** (fluxgate) heading of your vessel is shown on screen.

Note: The **Compass** heading is only displayed with **Automatic Off.** Remember the **Compass** reading may vary from the **COG** reading because **Compass** is where the vessel is pointing, and **COG** is where the vessel is going. For a vessel at rest the **COG** will vary wildly but the **Compass** reading will remain relatively steady.

Auto Pilot
Why Do I Need an Auto Pilot?

A marine autopilot (or pilot) is a mechanical, electrical or hydraulic system which maintains a vessel on a predetermined course without the need for human intervention. Using a direct or indirect connection with a vessel's steering mechanism, the marine autopilot relieves the crew from the task of manually steering the yacht. On sailing boats certain types of autopilot can be programmed to maintain a course defined at a pre-set angle to the wind or even auto tack.

The most basic marine autopilots are simply linked to an electronic compass and are set to maintain a fixed compass course. More sophisticated units incorporate processors which contain advanced software algorithms as well as an integral compass to combine position and navigation data from the GPS chartplotter with wind, speed and depth data from the instrument system. The result is smooth control of the boat's rudder providing accurate steering performance in all sea conditions.

Once the route has been activated in SeaClear or set by the helmsman, the marine autopilot takes over and guides the yacht between waypoints or other preset markers. Corrections to the autopilot's course can be made via SeaClear, the controls on the main unit.. The helmsman can override the autopilot at the touch of a button.

A marine autopilot enables the helmsman to take a break from steering his boat in order to rest or undertake other duties. Single handed sailors and short handed crews in particular find that marine autopilots are an essential piece of equipment.

Which Auto Pilot Do I Need?

There are many auto pilots on the market at widely varying prices. The simplest types are self contained and attach to your vessels tiller. More complex types control the helm via electric motors or hydraulic rams. The best type for you is dependant on your budget and your vessel be that motor or sailing.

Installing an Auto Pilot

Refer to the documentation supplied with your auto pilot. Pay particular attention to a reliable power supply, and site the auto pilot's fluxgate compass as near as possible to the centreline of the vessel and away from sources of magnetic interference.

If the auto pilot, or the autopilot computer has a serial input, and your computer does not have serial ports, you will have to purchase a "serial to USB" adaptor cable. If you need such a cable you have to install the correct driver.

As SeaClear outputs NMEA, your autopilot must be capable of inputting this data else you will have to install a suitable converter.

Carefully check the manufacturer's documentation to ascertain which input NMEA sentences your auto pilot needs for correct and safe operation.

Note: The helm must not be left unattended when SeaClear is connected to your auto pilot. Complex routes may cause your auto pilot to execute sharp turns to port or starboard which may prove hazardous.

Tutorial: Connecting an Auto Pilot using SeaClear,s NMEA Passthrough

In this tutorial you will configure SeaClear to output NMEA sentences to send data such as way points and routes to control your on board auto pilot.

1. From the **Tools** menu select **Properties** to open the **SeaClear Setup** window.

2. Select the **Comm** tab.

3. As we are outputting data using Passthrough from SeaClear, select the **Tx/Rx 1** tab.

4. Set the **PC Port Com** to the Com port the auto pilot is using..

5. Set the **BPS** (Bits per second) to **4800**.

6. In the **NMEA Output** area of the window check the check boxes of the NMEA sentence your autopilot needs Your auto pilot's documentation my list the sentences as **$ECAPA**, **$ECAPB** etc.

7. If your auto pilot need additional data such as GPS information enter ***** in the **NMEA Passthrough** data entry box. (The * tells SeaClear to pass through all NEMA sentences)

8. Click **Save** to save your settings.

Note: It is recommended that the next two steps are only taken *before* physically connecting your auto pilot. This ensures there is no erratic or hazardous movements of your vessel.

9. Activate your route and click **NMEA Out Off** to activate auto pilot output.

10. Check the setup is ok by selecting **Tools**, **System**, **NMEA Output Monitor**. The **NMEA Output Monitor** should display NMEA sentences being output from SeaClear. The auto pilot sentence to look for commence with **$EC**...

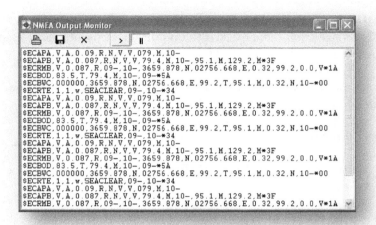

PolarCom
Why Do I Need Polar Com?

PolarCom, from Polar Navy, is part of a suite of navigation software that includes PolarView. PolarCom takes NMEA data and creates realistic on screen instruments either in digital or analogue form. PolarCom can be run independently from SeaClear to either overlay the SeaClear screen or be selected by using **Alt + Tab**. The instruments are easy to resize or display full screen so they are visible from the cockpit. PolarCom allows you to set alarms for Anchor, Depth, Arrival and Off Track (XTE Error)

PolarCom in full screen view

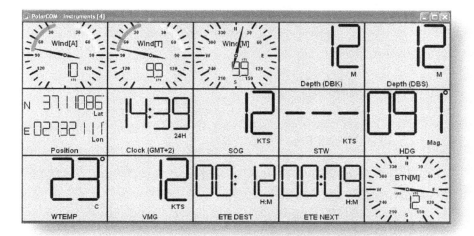

PolarCom in a reduced size.

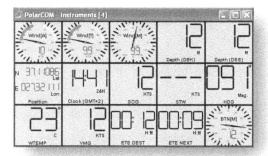

PolarCom set transparent and superimposed over SeaClear.

Installing PolarCom

Use the documentation from Polar Navy (http://www.polarnavy.com/index.php) to download and install PolarCom.

Tutorial: Connecting PolarCom using SeaClear NMEA Passthrough

You can use the NMEA passthrough feature of SeaClear to output on a COM port all NMEA data that is being received on other COM ports. In essence this means SeaClear is acting as a multiplexer and PolarCom is sees exactly the same NMEA data as SeaClear.

1. From the **Tools** menu select **Properties** to open the **SeaClear Setup** window.

2. Select the **Comm** tab.

3. As we passing on data from SeaClear select the **Tx/Rx 1** tab.

4. Set the **PC Port Com** to match a spare Com port.

5. Set the **BPS** (Bits per second) to **4800**.

6. In the **NMEA Output** area of the window enter * in the **NMEA Passthrough** data entry box. (The * tells SeaClear to pass through all NEMA sentences)

7. Click **Save** to save your settings.

8. Check the setup is ok by selecting **Tools, System, NMEA Output Monitor**. The **NMEA Output Monitor** should display NMEA sentences being output from SeaClear.

Tutorial: Displaying Instruments with PolarCom

In this tutorial you will set up PolarCom to receive NMEA data simultaneously with SeaClear and you will set up navigation instruments to be used alongside, or superimposed on SeaClear.

1. Double click the PolarCom icon on the Windows Desktop

2. Right click the PolarCom icon in the Windows Taskbar

3. Select **Configure**.

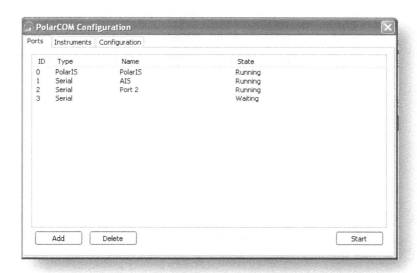

4. At the **PolarCom Configuration** window click **Add** to open the **Add Port** window.

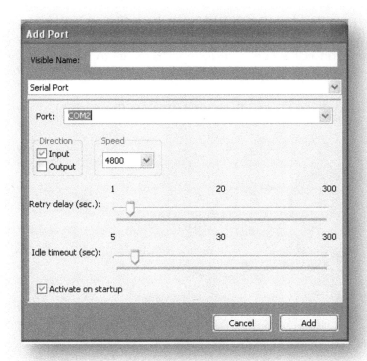

5. At the **Port** dropdown list select a port that matched the **TX/ Rx 1** port you setup in SeaClear.

6. Set the **Direction** to **Input** and the speed to **4800**.

7. Click the **ADD** button.

8. At the **PolarCom Configuration** window select the port you have just configured and click the **Start** button. If data is being received the port **Status** should change to **Running**.

9. Note Under some circumstances data may sop being received. If this is the case you may have to install two back to back virtual serial ports. Set SeaClear to ouput on one of these ports and Polar Con to receive in the other. Go to page 162 for installation instruction for virtual serial ports

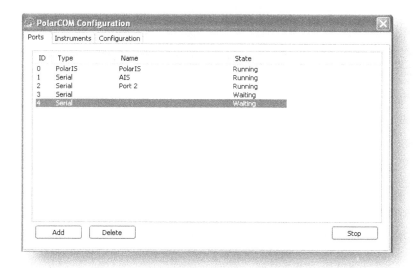

10. Select the **Instruments** tab and click the **Add** button to open the

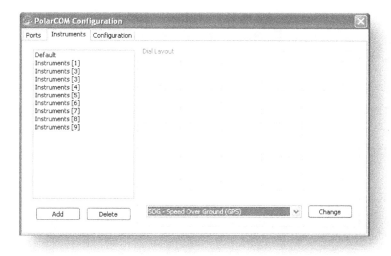

11. Select an **Instruments(?)** from the list.

12. In the **Dial Layout** areas of the window select a rectangle where a new instrument is to be positioned.

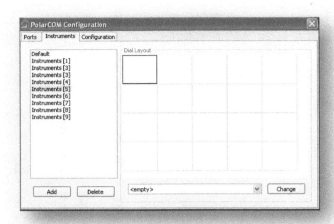

13. Select the instrument you wish to position from the dropdown list next to the **Change** button.

14. Click the **Change** button and your instrument is positioned in the selected rectangle.

15. Repeat this procedure to setup an instrument display to suit your needs. (Remember, certain instrument will need transducers to work correctly. e.g. If you have no wind transducer there is no point in creating a wind display instrument.

16. Close the window by clicking the close window **X.**

17. Right click the PolarCom icon in the Windows Taskbar and select the **Instrument** you have just created and it is displayed on screen.

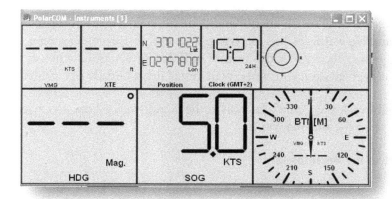

18. The instrument display can be repositioned by dragging its title bar, or resized by dragging borders or corners.

19. To make the instrument display transparent right mouse click and select **Transparent**.

20. To make the instrument display stay on top of other programs, such as SeaClear, right mouse click and select **Stay On Top**.

21. Other instrument displays can be created by repeating steps 9 to 15 above.

22. More than one instrument display can be shown on screen to simultaneously to create a multi display.

Tutorial: Setting up Depth and Anchor alarms.

In this tutorial you will set up anchor and depth alarms that when triggered, output distinctive audible warnings and. superimpose a visible warning in screen. As SeaClear has no anchor alarm, this feature of PolarCom is useful when at anchor to warn you, or even awaken you, when your vessel drags outside of a preset radius.

1. Right click the PolarCom icon in the Windows Taskbar and select **Alarms** to open the **Alarms** window.

2. Select the **Settings** tab .

3. At the **Depth** area of the window, check the **Minimum Depth Alarm** check box. Enter a value for the **Minimum Depth** and select the units as **Meters**.Enter your vessels **Draft** and the **Offset** of the transducer from the keel.

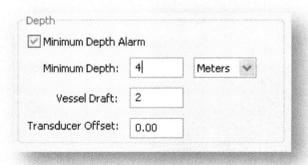

4. At the **Anchor** area of the window check the **Anchor Alarm** check box and set the Anchor Swing Radius and units as **Meters**.

Note: Set the anchor swing radius to a larger value than your actual anchor swing or false alarms result. In effect you are setting a ring fence around your vessel that if breached will trigger the anchor alarm.

5. If the water depth goes below the value set for the **Minimum Depth** the alarm is triggered with an audible signal and the **Alarm**s window is superimposed over your chart display. Dismiss the alarm by clicking the **Dismiss** button

6. If your vessel moves outside of the **Anchor Swing Radius** you have set the anchor alarm triggers with an audible signal and the **Alarm**s window is superimposed over your chart display. Dismiss the alarm by clicking **Dismiss**.

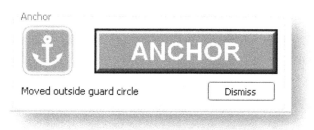

Setting a Vessel Anti-Theft Alarm.

You can use the **Anchor Alarm** in PolarCom as a vessel anti-theft alarm. If the vessel is at its mooring, or lying alongside, set the **Anchor Radius Swing** to about 10 m.(any less you may get false alarms) If the boat is broken into and moved the alarm will trigger when it leaves the 10m zone. If your PC is wired to an amplifier and an external speaker the audible alarm will deter most thieves or, at the very least draw attention to the vessel. Keep your PC in a secure location and secure access to your battery connections to make your alarm system tamper proof.

With a Bluetooth GPS receiver onboard your PC can be ashore whilst PolarCom monitors your boats position. You must be within range of your Bluetooth receiver (normally <10 m) or utilize a Bluetooth repeater with a range from 100m to 3000m. If you have a trailer sailor you can protect your vessel when it is parked on your drive or in your garage.

5. Using SeaClear Onboard

Choice of PC

The minimum specification for Pc to run SeaClear:

A PC running Windows XP/2000/NT or 95/98/ME. Several limitations in Windows 95/98/ME makesXP/2000/NT a better choice, avoiding several small problems and allowing much larger charts to work without problems.

800 * 600 resolution video. 1024 * 768 preferred, to fit all dashboard information.

Mouse USB or serial or Bluetooth.

One free serial port for the GPS. Or virtual COM port via USB.

Pentium+ or equal processor.

Min 32 Mb RAM memory. 64 Mb (depending on OS), is advised and will speed up chart loading.

10Mb free hard disk space. (4 Mb for SeaClear and 10K - 10 Mb for charts).

As can been seen in modern PC terms, the processor and capacity needs for SeaClear are very low. Most if not all recent PC's far exceed the specification needed for SeaClear.

Choice of Operating System

- Linux Running a simulator such as Wine

- Windows

- Mac Running a simulator such as Parallels or Desktop

Type of PC

The main choices are desktop, laptop or netbook

Locating the PC

You need the screen to be easily visible so most commonly the PC is located at the chart table. Most displays are not daylight readable so locate away from direct sunlight.

Securing the PC

The PC must be securely fixed so as not to slide when the vessel is heeling or in rough weather.

Protecting the PC

Pay particular attention to protect your PC from moisture such as rain or spray and lock it away in a dry locker when the vessel is unattended.

Power Considerations

The two main choices are use an invertor or a 12 volt adaptor. The adaptor is more efficient as unlike the inverter 12 volts is not converted to mains voltage and back to voltage for the PC. Some new net books are very frugal and only use about 5 watts and have a battery life between charges of up to eight hours.

The Ideal On Board PC?

Here is just one suggestion for the "ideal" on board PC.

Samsung NC10 NetBook:

• Low Cost	£250
• Low power requirements.	5 Watts.
• Long Battery Life.	6-8 hours.
• 130 Gb Storage	More than enough for SeaClear.
• Atom processor	Processor power switchable
• Windows XP	Stable.
• Bluetooth Mouse	No cable.
• Bluetooth GPS	No cable.
• Good 10" display	Brightness switchable.
• USB Ports	3 available
• Wi Fi	Built in.
• Other Ports	VGA and SD card.

6. Reference

Purchasing SeaClear Compatible charts from a Chart Digitising Service.

www.digital-charts.co.uk

Creating BSB Charts.

There is a free utility called Kapgen that converts from a calibrated tif image to the BSB format for use in such applications a Chart Navigator and Navigator Pro.http://www.dacust.com/inlandwaters/mapcal/index.html

Glossary of GPS Terms

- **AFE:** Atlas Florae Europaeae. The AFE grid is modified from the Military Grid Reference System (MGRS).
- **Antarctic Circle:** An imaginary circle on the surface of the earth at 66.5°S lat. or 23.5° north of the South Pole.
- **Arctic Circle:** An imaginary circle on the surface of the earth at 66.5°N latitude, or, 23.5° south of the North Pole.
- **BIPM:** Bureau International des Poids et Mesure. The international bureau of weights and measurements, in Paris. Responsible for the UTC time scale.
- **BRG:** Bearing. The compass direction from your position to a destination.
- **CDMA:** Code Division Multiple Access. a technology where different radio's can work on the same frequency. GPS uses it.
- **CODE PHASE GPS:** GPS measurements based on pseudo random code (C/A or P) as opposed to carrier of that code.
- **C Code:** The less accurate Civilian GPS Signal.
- **COG:** Course Over Ground, Your current direction of travel relative to a ground position (same as Track).
- **CONUS:** Continental United States. An abbreviation used in a class of Datums.
- **CTS:** Course To Steer.
- **CMG:** Course Made Good. How you are progressing towards your next waypoint.
- **Datum:** Map Datum's are the reference system used between the Lat/Longs and the map being used as a reference.
- **Dead Reckoning:** A very simple method of using time and distance to navigate.
- **Deviation:** Errors from your course. Either built in or unintentional. One type of deviation is magnetic, the difference between a true course and what a compass will tell you.
- **DGPS:** Differential GPS. A local transmitter is used for greater accuracy.
- **DBR:** Differential Beacon Receiver. Differential Beacon Receivers tune to the United States Coast Guard's high differential correction beacon stations for improved position accuracy.
- **Dithering:** The introduction of digital noise. This is the process the DOD uses to add inaccuracy to GPS signals to induce Selective Availability (SA).
- **DMA:** Defense Mapping Agency.
- **DOP:** Dilution of Precision, errors caused by bad geometry of the satellites.
- **DTK:** Desired Track. The course between To and From.
- **EGNOS:** The European WAAS.
- **EPE:** Estimated Position Error. How much the unit thinks it is off target.

- **Equator:** Zero degrees Latitude. A line around the center of earth 24,901.55 miles (40,075.16 kilometers) long.
- **ETA:** Estimated Time of Arrival.
- **ETE:** Estimated Time Enroute.
- **FGDC:** The Federal Geographic Data Committee (FGDC).
- **Fix:** A position that is determined by the navigation unit.
- **Galileo:** Europe's GPS system. May be operational by 2008.
- **GANS:** The Air Force's Global Access, Navigation, and Safety (GANS) program.
- **Geocaching:** The sport where you are the search engine, and you have to hunt for treasure caches with your GPS.
- **GDOP:** Geometric Dilution of Precision, see DOP.
- **Getting:** Ivan A. Getting, Father of the GPS.
- **GLONASS:** The Russian equivalent to the NAVSTAR GPS.
- **GMT:** Greenwich Mean Time or UT1 (Universal Time One) or UT is a time scale tied to the rotation of the Earth in respect to the fictitious 'mean Sun'. UTC is, however, kept within 0.9 seconds of UT1, by virtue of leap seconds.
- **GMAT:** Greenwich Mean Astronomical Time. Prior to 1925, in astronomical and nautical almanacs, a day of Greenwich Mean Time began at noon. This reckoning of Greenwich Mean Time is now called Greenwich Mean Astronomical Time, and is no longer used.
- **GPS:** Global Positioning System. Usually refers to the USA's NAVSTAR system.
- **Great Circle Route:** A great circle is defined as a circle on the earth's surface the plane of which passes through the center of the earth.
- **GS:** Ground Speed.
- **GWEN:** Air Force Ground Wave Emergency Network.
- **Handshaking:** coordination settings that allow or prevent communication between computer and a device.
- **Illumination:** The signal coming from the GPS Satellites.
- **Isogonic Lines:** A line on a map or chart where the magnetic deviation is the same.
- **ITU:** International Telecommunication Union.
- **JPALS:** Joint Precision Approach and Landing System, is a DGPS system pro rapid deployment. Uses WAAS/LAAS.
- **LAAS:** Local Area Augmentation System.
- **LDGPS:** Local Differential GPS. Two or more GPS Receivers are used to create a local reference to each other.
- **Magnetic North:** The direction to the Magnetic North Pole. It is what a magnetic compass indicates. It is different from True North, by the value of the Mag. Var.
- **Mag. Var.:** Magnetic Variation. the different between true North (pointing towards the geographic pole) and Magnetic North (pointing towards Magnetic Pole) where a compass points to.
- **Map Datum:** What reference map is used in determining the Fixes.

- **Map Projections:** A curved surface has to be "projected" onto a flat surface (the map paper). Mercator, Orthographic and Conic are common types of projections.
- **MCX:** Antenna connector used on some of the newer GPS units.
- **MGRS:** Military Grid Reference System. The MGRS is an alphanumeric version of a numerical UTM (Universal Transverse Mercator) or UPS (Universal Polar Stereographic) grid coordinate.
- **MOPS:** Minimum Operational Performance Standards.
- **MSAS:** The Japanese WAAS.
- **NANU's:** NOTICE ADVISORY TO NAVSTAR USERS.
- **NAD27:** North American Datum 1927. It is broken down into different areas, from Central America to Greenland.
- **NAD27 CONUS:** North American Datum 1927, Mean Value.
- **NDGPS:** Nationwide Differential GPS, The NDGPS plan calls for the conversion of a number of U.S. Air Force Ground Wave Emergency Network (GWEN) sites to broadcast DGPS signal. The range is 250 miles.
- **NEMA:** National Electrical Manufacturers Association.
- **NEMA 0183:** A communication protocol used by GPS units and other types of navigation and marine electronics.
- **NIMA:** National Imaging and Mapping Agency.
- **NSDI:** National Spatial Data Infrastructure.
- **OSM:** Ordnance Survey Maps. Britain's national mapping agency.
- **P Code:** Precision Code. The more accurate GPS signal.
- **PPS:** Pulse Per Second. Many receivers pulse their data at the top of every second facilitating timekeeping.
- **Prime Meridian:** The zero longitude location from where east and west is measured. It passes through Greenwich, England.
- **Pseudolite:** An extra satellites like device, installed on the ground in the local area. It is used to supply "illumination" and correction signals for DGPS systems.
- **Rhumb Line:** A line that passes through all meridians at the same angle. When drawn on a Mercator chart, the rhumb line is a straight line, because the Mercator chart is a distortion of a spherical globe on a flat surface. The rhumb line results in a longer course than a great circle route.
- **RNP:** Required Navigation Performance standards.
- **RS232:** The electronic voltage and timing interface definition for the connection of electronic equipment. Often used to connect NMEA devices to computers.
- **RTCM:** Radio Technical Commission for Maritime Services.
- **RTK OTF:** Real-Time Kinematic (RTK) On-The-Fly (OTF) positioning. A DGPS technique for high precision positioning of moving objects.
- **Serial:** Data that is sent one bit after another. A serial port on a computer is also called a COM port. See RS232.
- **SMG:** Speed Made Good. Marine term giving speed to waypoint taking into effect the course you are steering.

- **SOG:** Speed Over Ground.
- **SPS:** Standard Positioning Service (civilian GPS).
- **SA:** Selective Availability (intentional degradation of SPS). If they desire, the US military can turn off the accuracy of the GPS system.
- **SOIT:** FAA's Satellite Operational Implementation Team.
- **Statute Mile:** A unit of length equal to 5,280 feet or 1,760 yards (1,609 meters) used in the U.S. and some other English-speaking countries.
- **Track:** Your current direction of travel relative to a ground position (same as COG, Course Over Ground).
- **Triangulation:** by accurately measuring our distance from three satellites we can determine our position anywhere on earth.
- **Tropic of Cancer:** An imaginary circle on the surface of the earth at 23.5°N latitude.
- **Tropic of Capricorn:** An imaginary circle on the surface of the earth at 23.5°S latitude.
- **True North:** The direction to the geographic North Pole. It is different from Magnetic North, by the value of the Mag. Var.
- **USGS:** U.S. Geological Survey.
- **UPS:** Universal Polar Stereographic, a version of UTM.
- **USNG:** US. National Grid.
- **UTM:** Universal Transverse Mercator, A type of map projection. The grid lines you see on a USGS Quads represent a map projection known as Universal Transverse Mercator (UTM), and are 1000 meters apart.
- **UT or UT1:** Universal time or GMT (Grenwich Mean TIme) See GMT. It is different from UTC (difference can be almost 1 second). UT1 is the electronically distributed version. See also UTC for differences.
- **UTC:** Coordinated Universal Time. There are 7 Universal Times (all within 1 second of each other), and UTC is the "coordinated version of 'Universal Time'", hence the word order of Coordinated Universal Time. The abbreviation UTC is a language-independent international abbreviation, it is neither English nor French. It means both 'Coordinated Universal Time' and Temps Universel Coordonné. This is a time scale based on atomic clocks, by definition cesium clocks. UTC is the time basis for GPS.
- **VMG:** Velocity Made Good. Marine term. Effective velocity to waypoint taking into effect the course you are steering.
- **VOG:** Velocity Over Ground. Same as Ground Speed.
- **WAAS:** Wide Area Augmentation System.
- **Waypoint:** A navigation fix. Usually a destination or point of reference.
- **WGS84:** World Geodetic Survey 1984. A common map datum reference.
- **WRC:** World Radio Conference, an international conference where standards and interference issues are discussed.
- **Y Code:** P Code that has been encrypted.

Keyboard Shortcuts

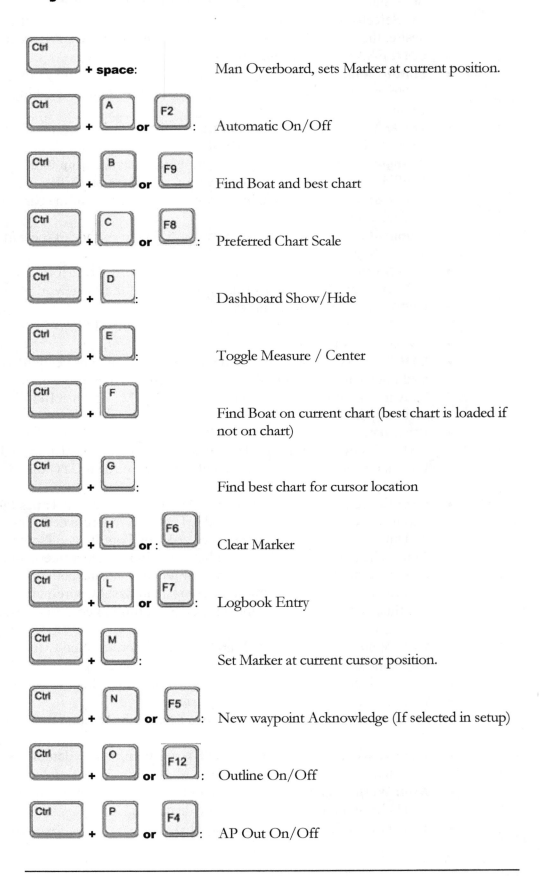

Ctrl + space: Man Overboard, sets Marker at current position.

Ctrl + A or F2: Automatic On/Off

Ctrl + B or F9: Find Boat and best chart

Ctrl + C or F8: Preferred Chart Scale

Ctrl + D: Dashboard Show/Hide

Ctrl + E: Toggle Measure / Center

Ctrl + F: Find Boat on current chart (best chart is loaded if not on chart)

Ctrl + G: Find best chart for cursor location

Ctrl + H or F6: Clear Marker

Ctrl + L or F7: Logbook Entry

Ctrl + M: Set Marker at current cursor position.

Ctrl + N or F5: New waypoint Acknowledge (If selected in setup)

Ctrl + O or F12: Outline On/Off

Ctrl + P or F4: AP Out On/Off

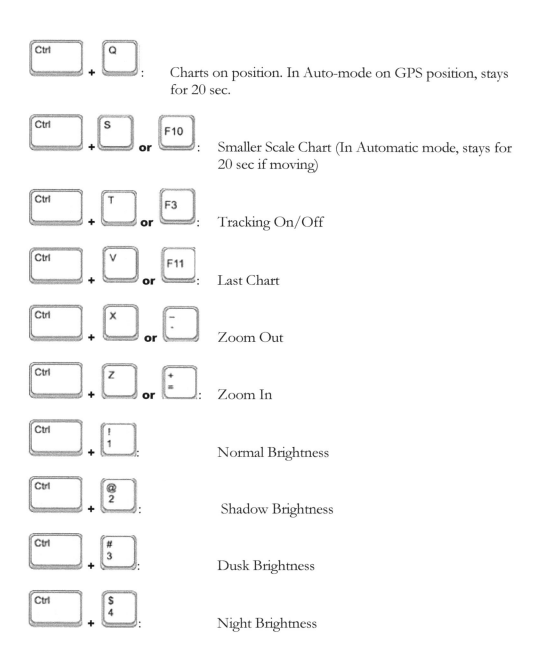

Ctrl + Q : Charts on position. In Auto-mode on GPS position, stays for 20 sec.

Ctrl + S or F10 : Smaller Scale Chart (In Automatic mode, stays for 20 sec if moving)

Ctrl + T or F3 : Tracking On/Off

Ctrl + V or F11 : Last Chart

Ctrl + X or − : Zoom Out

Ctrl + Z or + = : Zoom In

Ctrl + ! 1 : Normal Brightness

Ctrl + @ 2 : Shadow Brightness

Ctrl + # 3 : Dusk Brightness

Ctrl + $ 4 : Night Brightness

SeaClear Menus

Menus are context sensitive. In planning modes a top menu is available, where file loading and other not position related tasks are selected.

Popup menus, activated by the right mouse button, provide quick access to many functions, and the position where the menu is activated is used.

Normal planning mode top menu:
File menu
Chart:

List All. Show all charts in the Auto-load list.

Name Search: Opens the advanced search dialog.

Previous. Load previous chart.

Not Listed. Open chart not in the Auto-load list. Must be a calibrated chart.

Outline: Draw outline of all available charts on current chart. Only charts in the Auto-load database are outlined. Charts of same scale up to 2 - 50 * current scale (change in Setup) will be outlined. The outline is the border saved with the chart and will have the shape and direction as saved. If charts are grouped, only preferred charts are outlined.

Print Chart: Prints a hardcopy of current chart. Options for what to print include route, positions, track and outline. The Route and Position options have three states, when gray and checked text labels are not printed. The area to printed may be either the entire chart or what is currently visible on screen. The printer orientation is set to maximize the printed area, the setting from the printer is ignored.

Print list: Print a complete list of all charts including Lat and Long of corners and scale.

Route:

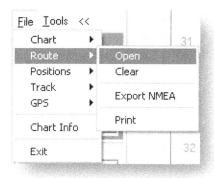

Open: Open a new route. Several routes may be selected, press Ctrl and select with mouse.

Clear:. Delete route from memory.

Export: NMEA. Sends all waypoints on the NMEA port as WPL and RTE records.

Print: Prints a hardcopy of the loaded routes.

Position:

Open: Several files may be opened, press ctrl and select with mouse. Note that duplicate names are not possible, only first occurrence will be loaded.

Save:

Save As:

Clear: Clear all positions from memory.

Unlock. Allow selecting, dragging and deleting of positions (Not when Automatic On or route editing).

Delete Selected:

Import: Waypoint+ and G7ToWin file import.

Export: Waypoint+ and G7ToWin file export.

Export NMEA: Sends all positions on the NMEA port as WPL records.

Print: Prints a hardcopy of all loaded positions.

Track:

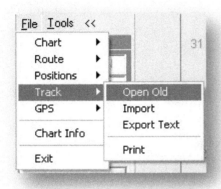

Open Old Track: Opens previously saved track and displays it.

Import: Converts a Waypoint+ or G7ToWin Track file to SeaClear format.

Export Text: Save the currently displayed track as a comma delimited text file. Time, position, speed and depth are saved. Positions are saved in decimal degrees for easy import in other programs.

Print: Prints a hardcopy of the loaded track. May be an active or old track.

GPS:

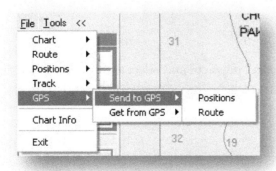

This menu is only enabled if G7ToWin is available.

Send to GPS – Positions or Route. Send loaded data to the GPS.

Get from GPS – Positions, Route or Track. Get data from the GPS.

Chart Info:

Show information on the current chart.

Exit:

Close SeaClear.

Tools Menu
Night Mode:

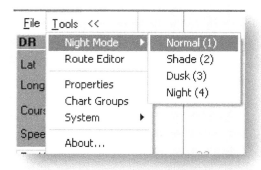

Select shading level. 1 is no shading, 4 is max.

Route Editor:

Open the route editor.

Properties:

Open the properties dialog.

Chart Groups:

Open the chart group organizing dialog.

System:

NMEA Input Monitor. Toggle NMEA input monitor window on/off.

NMEA Output Monitor. Toggle NMEA output monitor window on/off.

About...

Opens the **About SeaClear** window.

>>

Folds the dashboard to make all of the screen available. To Display the dashboard move the mouse over the edge.

Route planning top menu:
File menu
Route:

Open: Open a new route. Several routes may be selected, press Ctrl and select with mouse.

Save: Save to current filename. If several routes are open, no filename is set.

Save As: Save as new route.

Import Track: Import a previously saved track.

Import: Waypoint+ and G7ToWin file import.

Export: Waypoint+ and G7ToWin file import.

Export NMEA: Send WPL and RTE records to connected NMEA listener.

List Route: Opens a browsing window displaying all waypoints.

Reverse: Make the start point the end of the route.

Clear Route: Removes all waypoints.

Print: Prints a hardcopy of the loaded routes.

Open Chart:

List All: Show all chart registered in the autoload list.

Last: Open previously open chart.

Not Listed: Open chart not in the autoload list.

Outline: Toggle outline on/off. Only charts in the Auto-load database is outlined.

Open Positions:

Open a new Positions database.

Close Editor.

Popup Menus

The right mouse button activates Popup menus. The position where it is activated is used for SeaClear MMV 14 position dependant functions. Some functions from the top menu are duplicated for quick access.

Main popup menu

Preferred Charts:

Select preferred scale you like in both automatic and planning mode and preferred chart groups when double-click to select best chart. If automatic mode is on, the autoload preferred groups are displayed. Closest scale will be chosen. Use Up / Down key to change, 'M' sets to max scale, Esc closes without changing. "Best Chart" in menu still selects largest scale chart found.

Charts:

(Not available in AUTOMATIC mode).

Best Chart: Find and load best chart based on the current position.

Find Boat: Find best chart for ship.

Smaller Scale: Selects chart on same position but in smaller scale.

Previous: Swap back to previous chart.

On Position: All charts spanning the current position are listed.

Search: Opens the advanced search dialog.

All Charts: All installed charts are listed.

Routes:

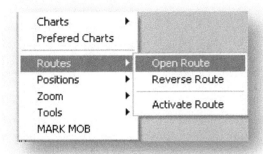

Open Route: All saved routes are listed.

Reverse Route: Reverse the route, putting the starting waypoint as the last.

Activate Route: Activate the route and show the route informationbox on the dashboard.

Positions:

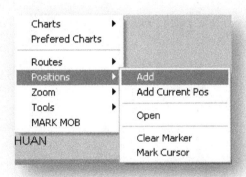

Add: Add a waypoint at current cursor position.

Add Current Pos: Add a waypoint at current Ship position.

Set Marker: Set the marker at the current mouse cursor position.

Clear Marker: Remove the mark.

When the mark is set, the "Marks/Cursor" panel will display the position, distance and heading from the ship.

Zoom:

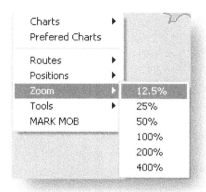

Zoom to fixed %. On some systems, zooming will slow down display updating dramatically, on others it is instant.

Tools:

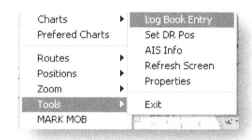

Log Book Entry: Make a manual log book entry.

AIS Info: Display information on nearest AIS target.

DR Update: Opens the Dead Reckoning input window. No use if a GPS is connected.

Refresh: Refresh the screen.

Properties: Open the system setup window.

Exit: Leave SeaClear.

MARK MOB:

Set the marker at the current boat position.

Route Popup Menu

When the right mouse button is pressed in the route editor, the following selections are available:

Best Chart: Find the best chart for the mouse cursor position.

More Charts: List other charts.

Extend: All waypoints will be appended.

Zoom: Set zoom level.

MapCal Menus
File Menu.

Open Image: Opens any image file, if cal data is available it is loaded.

Open From List: Find file by name, uses the Auto-load file.

Save Calibration: Saves calibration data (If it exists).

Edit menu:

Chart Information: Open the chart general info dialog. Enter scale, projection and chart datum, rest is optional. See step 4 above. Auto opens on new images.

Tools menu:

Convert :menu is for converting images format.

Convert ->Current to WCI: Converts loaded image to WCI format, including calibration.

Convert ->Current WCI to BMP: Converts loaded WCI image to BMP format, including calibration.

Convert->Single file to WCI: Most image types can be converted to WCI, including many formats that cannot be opened by MapCal or SeaClear. Images may be un-calibrated.

Convert->Images in Dir to WCI: Converts all image files in a directory.

Images may be un-calibrated, as calibration may be changed on WCI files.

Convert->MAP in Dir to WCI: Convert all OziExplorer MAP and image files to calibrated WCI files.

Import Cal menu is for importing calibration data to a usable format.

Import Cal->Old SeaClear Calibration: Imports all found chart calibrations. Paths must be set andseachart.dir must be in the current directory. Any existing new calibrations are overwritten.

Import Cal->CHI Calibrations: Imports all calibration data from a WinGPS .chi file.

Autoload List menu is for updating the SCAINDEX.BIN file.

Autoload List->Scan for New Charts: Scans for new charts in chart path.

Autoload List->Update: Scans for changed calibrations and check for new in chart path. Any charts not found will be left as is (in case you have a CD path and the CD is not inserted).

Autoload List->Recreate Erases SCAINDEX.BIN and generates new, scanning all directories in the chart path. Only charts found will be in the list.

Maintenance.

Remove Unused Calibrations: Removes any dormant calibrations remaining when images without embedded calibration data are removed from a directory.

Set Directories is used for setting all file path used by MapCal and SeaClear.

Set Directories: Set up all path needed. Updates the SEACLEAR_2.INI file.

<<

Folds the panel to the left edge and maximize the work area.

To display the panel again, move the mouse over the left edge.

Changing the SeaClear Default Settings (Configuration)

Display

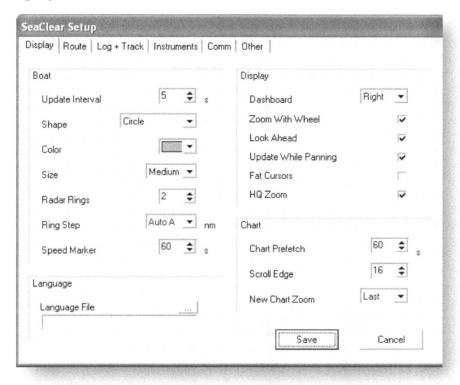

Boat:

Update interval: Screen update interval for the boat

Shape: Type of boat marker.

Color: Color of boat and speed mark.

Size: Size of boat marker.

Radar Rings: Number of visible radar rings.

Ring Step: Step between rings, or select Auto for adaptive step. Adapts to fit screen.

Speed Marker: Number of seconds ahead for the speed mark. Set to 0 to turn off.

Language:

Language file: Select file containing language. See Language section.

Display:

Dashboard: Left or Right side.

Zoom with wheel: On/Off.

Look-ahead: On/Off to position most of the screen ahead of the ship. If set to off the chart is positioned with the ship in the middle of the screen.

Update While Panning: (Disk mapped files) Update display while dragging with mouse.

Fat Cursors: Use bigger size more visible screen cursors.

HQ Zoom: Zoom out with more details. Slower on some systems.

Chart:

Chart Prefetch: Number of seconds to look ahead for best chart in Automatic mode.

Scroll Edge: Border of chart where mouse double-click will look for best chart.

New Chart Zoom: 100% or Last.

Route

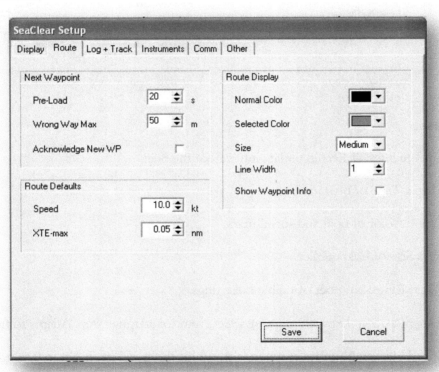

Next Waypoint

Pre-Load. Time before arrival to waypoint when next waypoint is activated.

Wrong way max. If the ship is taking a different path than the route, the distance the current waypoint may move in the wrong direction before the route is re-activated, finding a new start of the route.

Acknowledge New WP: If checked, route panel will turn red until acknowledged. Acknowledge with right-click menu on route panel or Ctrl + 'N' on keyboard.

Route Default

Default Speed: The default speed entered in a new waypoint.

Default XTE: The default XTE max error entered in a new waypoint.

Route Display

Normal Color: Color for normal display of waypoints.

Selected Color: Color for highlight display of waypoints.

Size: Marker size.

Line Width: Connecting line width.

Show Waypoint info. Show waypoint name on chart if available.

Log + Track

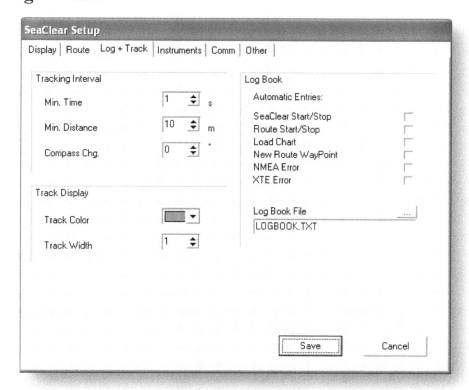

Tracking Interval:

Changes how often the boat position is written to the trace file.

Min Time. Between each trace. 0 to disable.

Min Distance. In meters. 0 to disable.

Compass change. In degrees. 0 to disable.

All parameters not 0 must be exceeded before a new position is written.

Track Display:

Track Color.

Track Width.

Log Book:

Automatic Entries. What will be added to the logbook automatically.

Log Book File. File to save the logbook.

Instruments

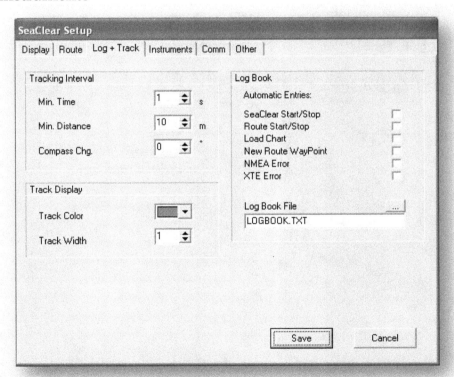

Depth Display:

Show depth: On/Off.

Depth Alarm. If the depth is less than this, the depth panel will alarm.

Trans. Depth: Depth location of transducer. Added to depth before displayed.

Wind Display.

Show wind information: On/Off.

Arrow Color: Select color for the arrow on the chart indicating direction and strength. 0-1 M/s it is dashed, 1-4 it is solid thin, 4-8 it is 2 pixel wide, 8-12 it is 3 pixel wide, >12 Fat 4 pixel wide arrow.

Compass Display:

Shows data from connected NMEA compass.

Log Data:

Use GPS for log and trip calculation.

Show Log and Trip. Added data is displayed on the GPS panel. If grayed, in auto mode only.

Log Cut Off. If speed is less, Log, Trip and Time will not be updated.

AIS:

Show AIS Targets: Turn AIS decoding on/off.

Show AIS Panel: Show AIS panel on dashboard (not shown in automatic mode).

Show AIS Labels: Show target names on chart.

CPA Max: Distance limit to show on chart CPA warning.

TCPA Max: Time limit to show on chart CPA warning. Set to 0 to disable.

Target Color: Color for AIS targets.

Target Size: Target marker size.

Comm

NMEA Connection:

PC Port. Com 1 - 9. 3 ports for receiving, 1 port for transmitting.

BPS: Bit rate setting. NMEA default is 4800.

GPS Datum:

The geodetic datum the GPS is set to. Select from list.

NMEA DR Update:

If GPS fails and NMEA data for speed and compass is available, it will update the DR panel. The dead reckoning calculation will be done by SeaClear to estimate positions until GPS is working.

NMEA Pass-through:

Messages received that shall be resent to output. Make sure messages generated by SeaClear are not passed through. Messages will be transmitted regardless of "NMEA OUT ON/OFF" setting.

NMEA Output:

When route is active and "NMEA OUT ON" is selected, calculated route data is transmitted.

Sentences: Select what to send to a Autopilot, radar or other NMEA listener connected, depending of the capabilities. WPL + RTE is only transmitted when a route isactivated, all other messages according to update interval setting.

If "Export NMEA" is used from File->Route or File->Positions, data will be transmitted regardless of NMEA Output settings.

Target Capabilities: How waypoint names are filtered before transmitted. "Upper Case" should work with most units accepting NMEA input. "+ Lower Case" allows ASCII below 128, "As Is" transmits all text as Windows ANSI standard 8 bit.

"Numeric" only sends waypoint numeric id and should work even with older units supporting NMEA input. This setting also affects what is transmitted with the route and position Export to NMEA and how text is saved with Waypoint+ and G7ToWin export. "Nexus" transmits in a Silva Nexus and NX2 format.

Update interval. How often the NMEA data is transmitted.

XTE Ampl. factor. The XTE-error sent to the autopilot may be amplified to provide better tracking, or lower, to avoid snaking. A value of 100% is 1:1.

NMEA Id. NMEA Talker Identification, always 2 characters. Normally "EC" or "GP".

Keep WP Id: On/Off. If on, fixed WP names will be used for all legs.

May be needed on some listeners. May cause listeners to switch to next waypoint without the need for acknowledge.

Other

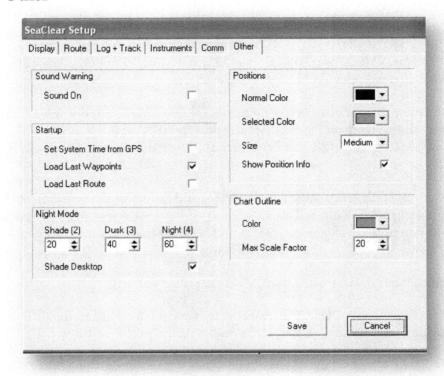

Sound Warning.

Uses the sound file specified in the .ini file as warning sound.

Startup:

Set system time. Use GPS. Updates the system time from the GPS at startup.

Load Last Positions: Loads positions from last session, even if not saved.

Load Last Route: Loads route from last session, even if not saved.

Positions:

Normal Color: Color for normal display of waypoints.

Selected Color: Color for highlight display of waypoints.

Size: Marker size.

Show Position Info. Show name on chart.

Night Mode.

Set the shading and what to shade.

Twilight, Dusk, Night: Set the of shading in % for each mode when selected.

A number from -95 to 95, where 0 is no shade and 95 the most. A negative number will invert the colors before shading.

Desktop: Also shade the Windows desktop.

Chart Outline.

Color: Changes color for chart outline.

Max Scale Factor: What to outline. If 20, charts in scale $1 - 20 *$ current scale will be outlined.

Help

SeaClear Video Tutorials
Links to Video Tutorials
These Tutorial Videos have been produced for the exclusive use of purchasers of SeaClear Unleashed in both hard copy, and downloadable versions. For access email acampb5160@aol.com with Video Access as the Subject and Code 728765 in the message You will be invoiced for 5 $. (for five video tutorials) On receipt of the payment your access will be set up within 24 hours.

Tutorial Video One: Connecting a GPS
Tutorial Video Two: Loading a Chart.
Tutorial Video Three: Calibrating a Chart
Tutorial Video Four: Set a Depth Alarm
Tutorial Video Five: Creating a Route

Accessing SeaClear Online Help
Some users may prefer online help to using a manual. **Online Help for SeaClear** is available at a small addition cost. Email acampb5160@aol.com with On Line Help Request as the Subject and Code 728765 in the body of the message. You will be invoiced for 10$. On receipt of the payment the details on downloading the **On Line Help for SeaClear** will be emailed to you within 24 hours.

FAQ's
Raymarine
Q: Can I use SeaClear with Raymarine equipment

A: Yes. Raymarine uses its own Seatalk data transfer method. SeaClear can be used with the use of a suitable adaptor See Seatalk on page 157

Linux
Q: Can I install and use SeaClear under the Linux Operating System?

A: There is no Linux version of SeaClear but, reports indicate that SeaClear installs and runs with no problems in the Windows emulator for Linux known as Wine.

Charts
Q: Can I create my own BSB charts?

A: There is a utility, Kapgen, that allows you to create your own BSB charts from a scanned image. You should be aware that this may infringe certain copyrights and or patents.

COM Ports

Q: SeaClear keeps reporting COM errors with this message. SeaClear correctly detects my GPS and plots the position. What is happening?

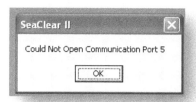

A: Whenever SeaClear opens, the COM ports set by the user are polled for data. When an unusable COM port setting is found the error message displays. Ensure that any inputs to SeaClear that are unneeded are set to 0 (zero) SeaClear will skip this port on start-up.

GPS

Q: I have connected my GPS to SeaClear and can see the NMEA data in the NMEA Output window but SeaClear does not display the current position.

A: Are you using your GPS simulator mode? Here is the sentence that SeaClear looks for to establish if the position is valid

...$GPRMC,023640,V,3730.1323,N,12228.9938,
W,0.0,0.0,221109,15.0,E,S*36,15.0,E,S*36

The 'V' '$GPRMC,023640,**V**,37...' tells SeaClear that the GPS signal is not valid. This must be due to the simulator mode. SeaClear is looking for '**A**' in this field. It will work OK outside with a clear sky view in normal mode.

Q: Should the GPS datum setting match the chart datum setting

A: The GPS datum setting should match the setting in your GPS, as that setting changes the NMEA position output. For modern GPS units it should be set to WGS84. SeaClear converts between GPS and chart datum; they do not need to match.

Q: I have a new BT-358 which I have connected to my laptop and desktop via a bluetooth dongle on each computer. The dongles are also new. I am just setting the computers to run SeaClear navigation software. Curiously, while the computers both pick up the signal from the BT-358, SeaClear's navigation screen keeps showing bizarre COG and SOG info. One second it shows a course of 350, the next 200, the next 084, etc. SOG shows as anywhere from O.O kts, to .3 or .4 kts. This happens when I am sitting perfectly still and have not moved in any direction.

A: This is perfectly normal. The accuracy of any GPS is only between 5 and 30 meters. Your GPS is reporting positions within this range even though you are stationary and interprets the differing positions as course, speed over ground etc.. All GPS units will give this effect. The effect disappears when you start moving a few meters.

Q: Mad mouse behaviour with GPS

A: This is a bug with Windows. The system is interpreting the GPS input as mouse movements. Below is the fix:

If you have a GPS receiver which can power up or down (e.g. chart plotters or hand held GPS units):

1. Start with your computer off.

2. Connect the GPS to your computer.

3. Turn on the power for your GPS unit.

4. Start your computer.

5. Wait until the mouse starts jumping.

6. Turn off the power to the GPS (i.e. shut down your GPS) but leave the GPS connected to the computer.

a. OPTIONAL - If there is a serial-to-USB adapter cable between your GPS serial port and the computer, you may disconnect the GPS from the serial-to-USB adapter cable. In all cases, leave the USB connector plugged in to your computer.

7. For Windows XP or Windows 2000:

a. Click Start

b. Right-click on My Computer

8. For Windows Vista:

a. Click Start

b. Right-click on Computer

9. Click Properties, a new window will open called "System Properties"

10. Click on the Hardware tab

11. Click the button labelled Device Manager, this will open a new window

12. A list of devices will appear.

13. Click on the "+" symbol to the left of "Mice and other pointing devices"

14. You should see listed a "Microsoft Serial Ballpoint"

15. Right-click "Microsoft Serial Ballpoint"

16. Click Disable

17. This will mark that device with a red X, and it should not bother you again.

18. Now you can close the Device Manager window.

19. Shut down your computer.

20. Reconnect the GPS (if disconnected)

21. Turn the power on for the GPS.

22. Start your computer.

23. You should have a stable mouse now.

AIS

Q. How do I connect a NASA AIS to SeaClear?

A: Follow the steps below:

1. Connect the AIS to the laptop (through the adapter)

2. If the AIS unit is receiving data then an LED in the adapter should flash occasionally; if there is no flash, check that your adapter has an LED.

3. Go to Device Manager on the laptop (depends on your OS but Control Panel -> System -> Hardware -> Device Manager is the route with XP).

4. In Device Manager listing look under Ports (NOT under Universal Serial Bus controllers) what devices are visible.

5. One of these should say something like USB-Serial Bridge and a COM number; note the number

6. .Right click this entry and go to Properties.

7. Under Port Settings set the Bits per Second to 38400; the other entries should not need changing.

8. Now open SeaClear select **Tools Properties** and the **Comm** tab.

9. Set the COM port to be whatever number you found at Step 4 above.

Q: What is AIS?

A: AIS or the Universal Shipborne Automatic Identification System (AIS) is a ship transponder system that is currently used by most of the commercial shipping industry. AIS uses two marine VHF channels. Each ship equipped with an AIS transponder sends out a packet every few seconds with information about the ship and its voyage. With an AIS receiver, you can pick up these radio signals and have them translated into a NMEA data sentence that can be accessed using a standard RS232 serial interface.

Q: Is it possible to connect my AIS receiver to a chartplotter?

A: More and more chart plotters are supporting AIS. At the time of writing, plotters from the following manufacturers feature AIS.

Furuno	Garmin
Standard Horizon	Raymarine E and C series
Interphase	Navman

Other manufacturers are working on this feature and have stated they will be able to support AIS in future models.

Q: What electronic chart programs can handle AIS?

A: Today several software packages support AIS. The ones known to work are:

PolarCom and PolarViewNS	EuroNav SeaPro
Rose Point Coastal Explorer 2009	Ytronic Yacht-AIS
Rose Point Coastal Explorer CE 2010	SeaClear
Nobeltec Visual Navigation Suite 8.0	DigiBOAT Software-On-Board
Nobeltec Admiral	Navicon AIS Navigator
Capn 8.0	COAA Ship Plotter
Boatcruiser 2.0	MaxSea with the Mobiles Module
Memory Map Navigator Pro	For the Mac, the recommended packages include:
Global Navigation Software NavPak	GPSNavX
ICAN Regulus	MacENC
Xanatos Titan	Polar View

Q: Will an AIS receiver work with manufacturer's proprietary data systems?

A: All networks that can handle NMEA VDM serial data at the speed 38400 baud will be able to handle AIS data. We have been informed that Silva and Navnet are able to do so. Raymarines, Seatalk and Simrad's Simnet currently do not handle AIS data.

Q: What are the basic steps to install an AIS receiver?

A: All AIS receivers essentially have the same four connections.

One connection is for a standard marine VHF antenna. This is usually via a BNC connector.

The second connection is NMEA position data input from either GPS/Chartplotter or your PC.

The Third is AIS Data output which is connected to your chartpotter/PC.

The forth connection is for 12 volt DC power.

Once these connections have been made, simply configure your chartplotter or PC software to utilize the output data stream. Note that AIS receivers use 38400 baud by default so make sure you configure your PC serial port and program appropriately.

The Comar CSB200 has the option of a dedicated GPS antenna, therefore not requiring NMEA input.

Q: I don't have a spare serial port on my computer. How do I connect an AIS receiver to my computer?

You have to use a serial to USB adaptor. Connect the serial end to the AIS receiver and the USB end to a spare USB port on your computer. Make sure you know which COM port has been assigned to the USB serial port and configure your software appropriately. Yachtbits can supply a suitable USB to RS232 adaptor, they can be found in the computing section.

Q: What type of VHF antenna do I need for an AIS receiver?

A: The VHF antenna should fulfil at least the following requirements:

Antenna type: Vertical radiator

Antenna gain: 0 3 dBd

Impedance: 50 ohm

Q: Can I use an existing marine VHF antenna?

A: Yes, you can use an existing VHF antenna on its own or you can use a splitter such as the EasyAIS Splitter to share one VHF antenna between your VHF/DSC radio and your AIS receiver. The EasyAIS Splitter also has an output for a FM stereo as well. While transmitting on the VHF radio, you may see some interruption of incoming AIS signals. Since AIS broadcasts from each ship are repeated every few seconds, this is not normally noticeable. Alternatively, use a dedicated AIS antenna. V-Tronix manufacture dedicated AIS antenna's optimised for AIS frequencies.

Q: What range should I expect?

A: Since AIS uses the same VHF frequencies as marine VHF, it has similar radio reception capabilities which is basically line of sight. This means that the higher your VHF antenna is mounted, the greater the reception area will be. Reception from ships that are 20 miles away on open water is not uncommon. Note that AIS has a major advantage over radar since it can see ships within radio reception range that are behind large objects, such as other ships or points of land. The USCGS has conducted test from SART aircraft and achieved AIS reception rages op up to 132 nm.

Q: What type of ships show up on an AIS display, and what doesn't?

A: Class "A" AIS is mandatory on all ships of 300 gross tonnage and upwards engaged on international voyages, cargo ships of 500 gross tonnage and upwards not engaged on international voyages and passenger ships irrespective of size. See the US Coast Guard web page on AIS for more information.

Other smaller commercial ships, such as fishing vessels, will equip themselves with Class B AIS transponders such as the Comar CSB200 voluntarily since there are major safety benefits to using AIS.

Naval ships are currently not required to carry AIS, neither small ships and pleasure craft (under 300tonnes!) Don't be misled by descriptions of "AIS Radar".

Q: I have hooked up my AIS receiver. Why don't I see ships immediately?

A: It normally takes a few seconds for ships to appear since the receiver needs to pick up a transmission from the remote ships transponders. The system allows for ships to rebroadcast their information every few seconds so within a minute you will typically see nearby ships appear on your navigation package.

Q: The ships show up as numbers? I thought I would also see the name of the ship.

A: Just wait. Ships broadcast voyage information every few seconds but also broadcast full ship information every 6 minutes. So after a few minutes, you should see complete information for every ship that the AIS receiver has picked up.

Q: So what kind of information is broadcast for each ship and how often is it updated?

A: A Class A AIS transponder broadcasts the following information every 2 to 10 seconds while underway, and every 3 minutes while at anchor:

MMSI number - unique referenceable identification

Speed over ground - 1/10 knot resolution from 0 to 102 knots.

Navigation status - at anchor, under way using engine or not under command

Position accuracy - differential GPS or other and an indication if RAIM processing is being used

Rate of turn - right or left, 0 to 720 degrees per minute

Longitude - to 1/10000 minute and Latitude - to 1/10000 minute

Course over ground - relative to true north to 1/10th degree

True Heading - 0 to 359 degrees derived from gyro input

Time stamp - The universal time to nearest second that this information was generated

In addition, the Class A AIS unit broadcasts the following information every 6 minutes:

MMSI number - same unique identification used above, links the data above to described vessel

IMO number - unique referenceable identification (related to ships construction)

Radio call sign - international call sign assigned to vessel, often used on voice radio

Name - name of ship, 20 characters are provided

Type of ship/cargo - there is a table of possibilities that are available

Dimensions of ship - to nearest meter

Location on ship where reference point for position reports is located

Type of position fixing device - various options from differential GPS to undefined

Draught of ship - 1/10 meter to 25.5 meters (note air-draught is not provided)

Destination - 20 characters are provided

Estimated time of Arrival at destination - month, day, hour, and minute in UTC

Q: Which VHF channels or frequencies are used with AIS?

A: AIS transponders and receivers use two VHF radio frequencies: 161.975 MHz (AIS1, or channel 87B) and 162.025 MHz (AIS2, or channel 88B). The USCG has asked the Federal Communications

Single channel switching receiver (NASA) and full time dual channel receivers (EasyAIS and Comar). What are the differences between these models?

All the units can receive AIS information from either AIS channel. The Nasa can only receive information on one channel at a time but automatically switches between both channels.

The EasyAIS and Comar units can receive all AIS broadcast information from both AIS channels simultaneously and consolidate the information from both channels into a single data stream. This generally means you will acquire new vessels sooner with the dual channel units and you will also get the full information about a vessel in a shorter period of time.

Q: If I am only receiving AIS information from one channel at a time, does this mean the NASA will not pick up the transponder broadcasts from half the ships in my area?

A: No,the AIS system uses two channels for redundancy. Ships broadcast information alternating between the two channels. Therefore, you will eventually pick up information on for every ship, even if the AIS receiver can receive on one channel.

Q: I want AIS and High Speed Heading inputs in to my Raymarine C/E series, how do I do it with only one NMEA Port?

A: You need a Actisense NDC-2 NMEA Data combiner. This combines the High Speed Heading Data and the AIS Data into a single data stream which can then be fed into the one port.

If you have two E Series, just feed the High Speed Heading in on one display and the AIS in on the other.

Q: Can I get more information on how the dual channel system works?

A: The best source for more information is to look at the documents related to the AIS standard. On the subject of dual channel support, the standard states:
The normal default mode of operation should be a two-channel operating mode, where the AIS simultaneously receives on both channels in parallel. In order to accomplish this performance, the AIS transponder should contain two TDMA receivers.

Channel access is performed independently on each of the two parallel channels.

For periodic repeated messages, including the initial link access, the transmissions should alternate between AIS 1 and AIS 2. This alternating behaviour is on a transmission by transmission basis, without respect to time frames

Transmissions following slot allocation announcements, responses to interrogations, responses to requests, and acknowledgements should be transmitted on the same channel as the initial message.

For addressed messages, transmissions should utilize the channel in which messages from the addressed station were last received.

For non-periodic messages other than those referenced above, the transmissions of each message, regardless of message type, should alternate between AIS 1 and AIS 2.

Base stations could alternate their transmissions between AIS 1 and AIS 2 for the following reasons:

To increase link capacity.

To balance channel loading between AIS 1 and AIS 2.

To mitigate the harmful effects of RF interferance.

Also the US Coast Guard site has the following information: Although only one radio channel is necessary, each station transmits and receives over two radio channels to avoid interference problems, and to allow channels to be shifted without communications loss from other ships.

Q: Where can I find out more specific information about AIS?

A: See the US Coast Guard site on AIS:
http://www.navcen.uscg.gov/marcomms/ais.htm

Thanks to KML Electronics Ltd 2000 for this Q A on AIS

Routes
Q: I am having trouble using the route editor to make a route for our local races. The trouble is keeping the race marks in order. The editor wants to rearrange them going to the next closest mark instead of in the order entered. Can anyone help?

A1: You should use the "extended" option in Route Editor.

A2: Put mark 1 then mark 2 then, create mark 3 well away from the track 1 -2 … so that it creates a track from mark 2 to 3 …. Then move the mark to where its wanted.

A3: When the next mark is close to more than one previous marks, then it may happen that the route concatenates the marks not correctly. The trick is the following: put the next mark enough close to the one you want the course follows, then, after the connection, move the new mark where you want.

Q: When I activate a route the second way point is highlighted and activated. Why is this.

A: When you activate a route SeaClear activates the first leg of the route and highlights the second way point. This is normal. SeaClear need the first leg activated in order to compute the XTE. SeaClear computes a course to minimise or eliminate the XTE. If an auto pilot is connected this may result in a sharp turn to port or starboard which may prove hazardous. In order to minimise this situation position the vessel as close a possible to the the first way point of a route *before* it is activated.

Seatalk
Q: My nav system uses the Seatalk data bus. I understand SeaClear only recognises NMEA. How can I use Seatalk with SeaClear?

A: Most Seatalk systems include limited NMEA outputs. Foe full data transfer to Seatalk, including AIS, you need a Seatalk to NMEA adaptor available from Raymarine and other marine electronic suppliers.

Display.
Q: When I open SeaClear some of the dashboard panels are missing In particular I cannot see the **Measure** and **Centre** buttons.

A: SeaClear automatically adjusts the dashboard display to accommodate the maximum amount of information. On some PCs, particularly net books the display area is too small. You may find the **Measure** and **Centre** button missing for this reason. For a full display you resolution must as a minimum 1024 by 768.

MapCal

Q: When I enter Lat, and Long values for a calibration point, then go on to enter another point, MapCal keeps changing the values on the point I just entered. Why is it doing this? How do I get it to leave the data I enter alone?

A: Make sure the Fix Lat Long box is checked and that you Activate each calibration point before moving on to the next.

Q: I have already set two **Calibration Points** for my map in MapCal. When I go to set the third and fourth points the **Lat Long** data has already been set. Why is this?

A: Once you have set two **Calibration Points** MapCal uses this data to predict the Lat and Long of any further points. This reduces time in entering the data for those points. Do not forget to click **Activate Changes** before moving on the next point and **Save Calibration** before exiting.

Chart Datums

Q: What is the WGS84 Chart Datum?

A: In the early 1980s the need for a new world geodetic system was generally recognized by the geodetic community, also within the US Department of Defense. WGS 72 no longer provided sufficient data, information, geographic coverage, or product accuracy for all then current and anticipated applications. The means for producing a new WGS were available in the form of improved data, increased data coverage, new data types and improved techniques. GRS 80 parameters together with available Doppler, satellite laser ranging and Very Long Baseline Interferometry (VLBI) observations constituted significant new information. An outstanding new source of data had become available from satellite radar altimetry. Also available was an advanced least squares method called collocation which allowed for a consistent combination solution from different types of measurements all relative to the Earth's gravity field, i.e. geoid, gravity anomalies, deflections, dynamic Doppler, etc.

The new World Geodetic System was called WGS 84. It is currently the reference system being used by the Global Positioning System. It is geocentric and globally consistent within ±1 m.

"When working with these or other map datums, it is important to always be aware of which datum a particular map is referenced in because often there are large differences in terms of distance between place to place on each different datum. This "datum shift" can then cause problems interms of navigation and/or in trying to locate a specific place or object as a user of the wrong datum can sometimes be hundreds of meters from their desired position."This is from http://geography.about.com/od/geographyintern/a/datums.htm A couple of other items I noted were:"Within the World Geodetic System (WGS), there are several different datums that have been in use throughout the years. These are WGS 84, 72, 70, and 60. The WGS 84 is currently the one in use for this system and _is valid until 2010. " It is 2010 now, so what happens next? Anybody know if they are going to use a new base ellipsoid for the next standard or simply extend the expiry date of the standard? and: "Similar to WGS 84 is the North American

Datum 1983 (NAD 83). This is the official horizontal datum for use in the North and Central American geodetic networks. Like WGS 84, it is based on the GRS 80 ellipsoid so the two have very similar measurements. NAD 83 was also developed using satellite and remote sensing imagery and _is the default datum on most GPS units today."

NMEA

Q: What is NMEA?

A: The NMEA-0183 standard has details for electrical specifications as well as protocol conventions. The electrical specifications actually recommend using the RS-422 standard which is slightly different than the RS-232 standard mentioned above. The RS-422 standard is a newer standard that specifies two wires each for transmitting and receiving for a total of four signal wires, while the older RS-232 standard specifies a common signal ground and one wire each for transmitting and receiving for a total of three signal wires. In most cases, an RS-422 signal coming from an electronic device will be able to be read by an RS-232 port on a computer.

The NMEA protocol is based on ASCII (American Standard Code for Information Interchange) characters being sent along the wire at 4800 bits per second or about 600 characters a second. Since any personal computer can read ASCII characters, it's easy to snoop on the NMEA transmission coming into your computer and see what it looks like. If you set up a direct connection to your COM port using Hyper Terminal (or a similar program), you see a stream of characters that looks something like this:

```
$GPGLL,4338.581,N,07015.101,W,170110,A*3D
$PGRMZ,4,f,3*1F
$PGRMM,WGS 84*06
$GPBOD,088.3,T,105.8,M,MANTIN,STHPTI*5B
$GPWPL,4347.000,N,06851.300,W,MANTIN*45
$GPRMC,170111,A,4338.581,N,07015.101,W,000.0,360.0,060199,017.5,W*73
$GPRMB,A,7.15,L,STHPTI,MANTIN,4347.000,N,06851.300,W,061.4,081.6,,V*1
B
$GPGGA,170111,4338.581,N,07015.101,W,1,00,2.0,1.1,M,-31.8,M,,*71
$GPGSA,A,3,,,,,,,,,,,,,2.7,2.0,3.0*36
$GPGSV,2,1,08,03,17,171,42,06,21,047,44,14,28,251,45,16,25,292,44*71
$GPGSV,2,2,08,18,13,315,41,22,83,222,53,25,44,086,48,29,12,147,40*7C
$PGRME,15.0,M,22.5,M,15.0,M*1B
```

Each line is called an NMEA sentence. Each sentence starts with a $, followed by a two character "talker ID". In this case, the $GP indicates that the signal is coming from a GPS (a Garmin GPS45). The next three letters indicate the type of sentence that is being sent. Some common sentences are:

APB - Autopilot format B
BOD - Bearing - origin to destination waypoint
BWC - Bearing and distance to waypoint - great circle
BWR - Bearing and distance to waypoint - rhumb line
DBT - Depth below transducer
GGA - Global Positioning System Fix Data

GLL - Geographic position, Latitude and Longitude
GSA - GPS dilution of precision and active satellites
GSV - Satellites in view
HDM - Heading, Magnetic
HSC - Command heading to steer
MTW - Water temperature
RMB - Recommended minimum navigation information
RMC - Recommended minimum specific GPS/Transit data
RTE - Waypoints in active route
VWR - Relative wind direction and speed
VTG - Track made good and ground speed
WPL - waypoint location
XTE - Cross track error, measured

Notice that a few lines start with a $P followed by a GRM. These are called proprietary sentences. Each manufacturer has the option of sending out sentence types that aren't necessarily part of the NMEA standard protocol. In order to do this, the device needs to start the sentence with a $P and then follow it by a manufacturer ID (GRM in this case denoted Garmin), and then send any data they choose after that. In the lines above you'll see three proprietary Garmin sentences:
GRM - E which denotes estimated error
GRM - Z which denotes altitude
GRM - M which denotes map datum.

So by looking at the first line of the transmission, you can see a valid sentence being sent by a GPS ($GP), giving our geographic position in latitude and longitude (GLL), at 43° 38.581' North (4338.581,N), 70° 15.101' West (07015.101,W) at 17:01:10 UTC (170110). The last few characters indicate the validity of the data and include some error checking to make sure that the transmission wasn't garbled.

Links to Resources

NOAA: http://www.noaa.gov/

Yachtua: http://www.1yachtua.com/

BSB to Tif: http://libbsb.sourceforge.net/

PolarNavy: http://www.polarnavy.com/index.php

Franson Gate: http://franson.com

Worldwide digital charts www.digital-charts.co.uk

Yahoo User Group: http://groups.yahoo.com/group

Google: http://www.google.com

Kapgen: http://www.dacust.com/inlandwaters/mapcal/index.html

Linux: http://www.linux.org/

Wine: http://www.linux.org/apps/AppId_3538.html

Virtual Serial Ports: http://mixw.net/index.php?j=related

Installing Extra Virtual Serial Ports.

There may be times when you run out of serial ports. This free utility will create paired serial ports. Paired means you can input data on one COM port and read the same data on another COM port.

1. Download the utility **ComEmulDrv3.zip** from:

http://mixw.net/index.php?j=related

2. Unzip the file to a temp directory.

3. Open **Control Panel** from Windows and select **Add Hardware**.

4. In **Add Hardware Wizard** box, click **Next**.

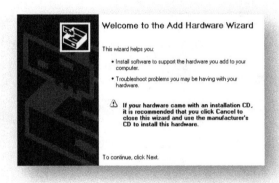

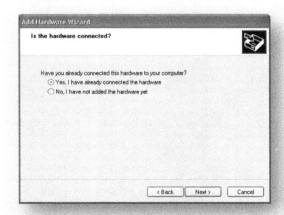

5. Check **Yes, I have already connected the hardware** " Click **Next**.

6. From Hardware types list, select "Add a new hardware device " and click "Next"

7. Choose "Multiport serial adapter"

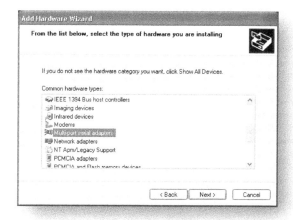

8. Choose MixW serial port bridge

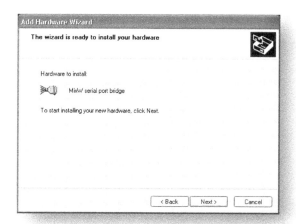

9. Click "Have Disk"Click "Browse" and locate **ComEmulDrv.inf file**, from temp folder you unzipped to earlier and click "Open"(download driver to prepared folder) (CD drive :\TNCemulation\driver\ComEmulDrv.inf)

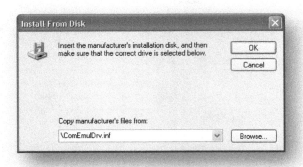

Ignore the warn ing and click "**Continue Anyway**"

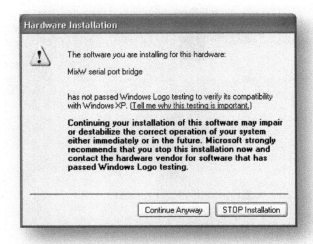

10. Click "**Finish**"

Tuning COM ports

11. Open "System" from Control Panel

12. Select "**Hardware**" tab

13. Click "Device Manager" Locate "MixW serial port bridge" under "Multi-port serial adapters"

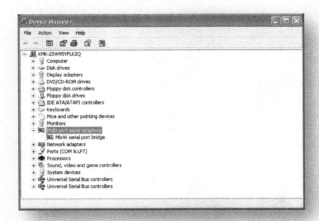

14. Right-click on MixW serial port bridge and choose "Properties" Select Properties tab Choose first and second emulated ports for each pair (COM4 and COM5)

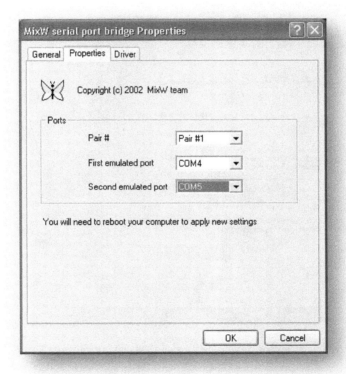

WARNING: Choosing ports which already exist may cause driver conflicts!

15. Click **OK** and reboot the computer

16. Emulated ports are now ready to use.

Acknowledgements

The author of SeaClear would like to thanks the following people:

- Ollie for writing a superb navigation system and making if freely available to all.

- The following people for proof reading and advice and encouragement.

  - Anne

  - Mike Robinson .

  - Don.

  - Steve .

- The userS at http://groups.yahoo.com/group/seaclear_mapping/

- The SeaClear users at: http://www.cruisersforum.com/forums/

- My wife Anne for proof reading and bottles of beer.

- Musti my dog for not eating the draft copies.

- The publishers for allowing me to publish this work.

- Digital-charts.co.uk who have supplied charts for creating screenshots.

- And finally to those people who have put information on the internet and whose copyrights are too numerous to mention.

Index

www.ingramcontent.com/pod-product-compliance
Lightning Source LLC
Chambersburg PA
CBHW081226050326
40689CB00016B/3697